JANE'S POCKET BOOK OF AIRSHIPS

ALSO AVAILABLE IN THIS SERIES:

JANE'S POCKET BOOK of COMMERCIAL TRANSPORT AIRCRAFT
JANE'S POCKET BOOK of HOME-BUILT AIRCRAFT
JANE'S POCKET BOOK of LIGHT AIRCRAFT
JANE'S POCKET BOOK of MAJOR COMBAT AIRCRAFT
JANE'S POCKET BOOK of MAJOR WARSHIPS
JANE'S POCKET BOOK of MILITARY TRANSPORT and TRAINING AIRCRAFT
JANE'S POCKET BOOK of MISSILES
JANE'S POCKET BOOK of MODERN TANKS and ARMORED FIGHTING VEHICLES
JANE'S POCKET BOOK of NAVAL ARMAMENT
JANE'S POCKET BOOK of PISTOLS and SUB-MACHINE GUNS
JANE'S POCKET BOOK of RESEARCH and EXPERIMENTAL AIRCRAFT
JANE'S POCKET BOOK of SPACE EXPLORATION
JANE'S POCKET BOOK of SUBMARINE DEVELOPMENT

TO COME:

JANE'S POCKET BOOK of RECORD-BREAKING AIRCRAFT
JANE'S POCKET BOOK of REMOTELY PILOTED VEHICLES
JANE'S POCKET BOOK of RIFLES and LIGHT MACHINE GUNS

JANE'S POCKET BOOK OF AIRSHIPS

LORD VENTRY AND EUGÈNE M. KOLEŚNIK

COLLIER BOOKS
A Division of Macmillan Publishing Co., Inc.
New York

Macmillan Publishing Co., Inc.
866 Third Avenue, New York, N.Y. 10022
Collier Macmillan Canada, Ltd.

Library of Congress Catalog Card Number: 73-15287

First Collier Books Edition 1977

Second Printing 1977

Printed in the United States of America

Contents

This stereoscopic slide is over one hundred years old, and is probably the oldest in existence showing a winged aircraft. The subject depicted on the stereo photographs is Frederick Marriott's *Avitor*, which was a combination of airship and aeroplane. The *Avitor* was flown in California in 1868

Foreword

The main work in the development of airships was done half a century and more ago — and yet the potential of airships with improved modern materials and techniques is enormous. Even forty years ago, Zeppelins were crossing the oceans to timetable, facing all weathers, but today, airships can do even better, operating from mooring masts and capable of surviving gales gusting over 80 m.p.h. In the past, airships required large and costly handling parties but since 1921 when the late Major G.H. Scott introduced the high mast, the techniques of mast mooring and mechanised ground handling have developed to the point where even the largest airships can be dealt with by a handful of men, in winds of up to 20 m.p.h.

Gas diffusion in the old ships used to be more than 100 per cent a month. Today, with synthetic fabrics, this figure can be reduced to not more than 2 per cent. The latest fabrics are also very much lighter so providing improved performance with no loss of strength. For example, an envelope of 100,000 cubic feet, weighing just over 1,800 lb in 1918, would probably weigh between 600 and 700 lb today.

With speeds of under 10 m.p.h., the very early airships lacked steerage way and could only ascend in an almost dead calm — when climbing and descending, the pilots handled their ships as free balloons. As gas was relatively cheap, the pilots of the hydrogen ships used to 'valve' (release gas) especially if light on landing. Modern pilots would only valve costly helium in an emergency. So, to avoid arriving light due to the burning of fuel and superheat, modern airships taxi off the ground and often land like aeroplanes, making full use of dynamic lift. Although the technique was perfected in America, the British were the first to make use of dynamic lift. The early ships were fitted with swivelling propellers and so used helicopter technique.

Where sheer speed is required, airships have few possibilities; but there are many areas in which they can do a better job than heavier-than-air machines — and this is where their future lies. The Zeppelin engineers, with their projected *LZ 132* suggested a maximum speed of 100 m.p.h. This would make such an airship three times as fast as the fastest ocean liners and would be fast enough for many purposes. For cargo-carrying, the large rigid can obviously transport items of a far more bulky nature than the largest aeroplanes — and cargo carrying need not involve excessive speed.

Only the large rigid airship can give the aerial passenger the same sort of comfort as an ocean liner. Anyone who has flown in the Zeppelins and now in the modern jets, knows how standards have fallen. Very little pleasure remains in travelling in the so-called air liners of today.

When safety is considered, the airship scores again. A modern rigid would be virtually fire-proof when helium-inflated and diesel driven. Unlike the aeroplane, it can remain airborne with all power units stopped — and so "feel" its way through fog. Crew members can climb about a rigid airship, even in flight, and this means that, if running repairs are required, they can be carried out immediately — an additional safety factor. Where comfort and safety are concerned, the airship scores every time — and it does not require the elaborate and costly blind landing systems essential to modern jet aircraft.

Environmentally, airships have everything to offer. They use comparatively little fuel, they need no vast elaborate airports and lengthy ground-consuming runways and, above all, they are quiet.

They make much better neighbours than jets.
The smaller, non-rigid airships are ideal for two widely-differing purposes: advertising and the escort of convoys in war. At the moment, the development of airships is almost wholly in the public relations field but the vital role that airships can play in convoy escort should be recognised. No convoy under close airship escort suffered loss in war from mine or U-boat. Non-rigids should be developed and flown as part of our defence programmes, and also used to train crews for all types of airship. They could also be used to test materials to be employed in the rigids of the future.

Originally we owe the non-rigid to France and the rigids to Germany — while Italy was first with the semi-rigids. Britain developed the Eta patch suspension, the utilisation of propeller slip-stream for pressure control, swivelling propellers and the mooring mast — and indeed pioneered mooring-out generally. So several countries have all played their part in the development of the airship — as this book will show.

VENTRY

Introduction

The era of lighter-than-air craft began in 1873 with the flight over Paris of the Montgolfier brothers' hot-air balloon. However, the Montgolfiers' monopoly was short-lived for the first flight of a hydrogen-filled balloon, made of rubberized fabric, was to take place a few months later at the Tuileries on 1 December 1783. Not long afterwards the more practical nature of the hydrogen balloon came to the attention of the military authorities, and by 1794 a French balloon, the *Entreprenant*, was used for reconnaissance work. At that time Coutelle and Conte formed two companies of *aérostiers* and used them with some considerable success in military operations. Napoleon disbanded these companies in 1799, mainly because they were not mobile enough.

Although many practical designs were promulgated and a few successful airship models flown, it was not until 1884 that the first real dirigible craft was flown. This ship was *La France* of Captain Charles Renard and Arthur Krebs, which made a round trip, returning to the point of the ship's departure. *La France* had a bamboo gondola which was 108 feet long. A large canvas-covered propeller fixed in the nose was powered by an electric motor designed by Captain Krebs. This motor developed 8 h.p. at 3,600 r.p.m., but reduction gears reduced the propeller speed to 50 r.p.m The motor was powered by banks of batteries weighing almost 900 pounds. The motor itself weighed 211 pounds, thus overloading the craft, so in 1885 the original power unit was replaced with a 9 h.p. Gramme bipole dynamo. *La France* was 165 feet long, with a maximum diameter of 27.5 feet. The volume of the envelope was approximately 66,000 cubic feet. The maiden flight of *La France* was carried out over the balloon park at Chalais-Meudon on 9 August 1884.

To give full details of the partial successes of the early airship pioneers would require more space than we are allowed in this book, but the very importance of their contribution to the development of the airship precludes us from making no mention of the efforts of these intrepid men. The main reason why so many attempted dirigible flights failed, was that the craft were underpowered and of poor aerodynamic shape. Often craft were designed to be rowed like a boat through the air, and had such fanciful design as to be totally impracticable. The helicoidal craft designed by Pierre Ferrand in 1835 is a good example of the fantastical projects produced by a feverish imagination.

However, the scientific synthesis of aerodynamics and aerostation produced some outstanding craft. For example in 1850 Hugh Bell flew a small elongated craft at Vauxhall in London. This ship was 55 feet long, with a volume of 17,700 cubic feet. It made only two flights, as human muscle, its motive power, proved inadequate.

Also in 1850 Pierre Jullien, a clockmaker, demonstrated a scale model, 23 feet long, of a craft he was to build in 1852. The model had two airscrews driven by a clockwork motor which actually enabled it to be flown against a moderate wind. The full scale ship built by Jullien, *Le Précurseur*, although of reasonable design, was never flown. It is interesting to note that *Le Précurseur* was of an asymmetric shape, with the circumference of the envelope increasing towards the nose and decreasing towards the tail. This was a most successful aerodynamic form, and was to be generally adopted by airship builders a century later.

The steam powered dirigible built by the inventer Henri Giffard was perhaps the most important craft before Renard and Krebs flew *La France*. It was 144 feet long, with a diameter of 39 feet, and a volume of 88,000 cubic feet. A 3 h.p. coke-fired steam engine drove a three-bladed airscrew at 110 r.p.m., and the exhaust gases were directed downwards in order to eliminate the risk of fire from a stray spark. Giffard's ship was of good design, enabling changes of course, and even full circles to be made, using a simple rudder to steer the craft.

Several abortive attempts were made in America to harness steam to propel balloons and airships, but only in 1868 did these efforts meet with success in the shape of Frederick Marriott's *Avitor*. The *Avitor* was a steam-powered craft promoted by The Aerial Steam Navigation Company, which was founded and funded to the tune of 1 million dollars by Mr Marriott, a San Franciscan publisher. The craft, a powered combination of balloon and glider, carried out a number of flights.

In 1872 Paul Hänlein built a craft with a volume of 85,000 cubic feet. This ship was 165 feet long, 30 feet in diameter, and incorporated a ballonet under an envelope supported by a long structure which also distributed the loads and forces acting on the envelope. This craft only 'flew' on the end of a cable, but quite good results were obtained. Also in 1872 an 8 h.p., 28,000 cubic feet craft was tested by a Dr Wölfert. The craft, known as the *Deutschland*, burst into flames and crashed while on a flight at Tempelhof, killing Dr Wölfert and Herr Knabe, its mechanic. The next most serious attempt was the airship constructed by the French naval architect Dupuy-de-Lôme during the siege of Paris. However, the muscle-power provided by eight strong men proved insufficient, and the craft is now only significant for the space it occupies at the Musée de l'Air at Chalais-Meudon.

Real genius can inspire, and point the way to a new style, and the critics and imitators of this genius can draw on its inspiration and achievements to create new rules, and from them a whole new technology. Thus, it was from the dedicated application of the ideas of Count Ferdinand von Zeppelin and a few other visionaries that the airship 'industries' were fabricated. Count Zeppelin may not have been a technologist, but despite numerous setbacks he had the courage and tenacity to apply the skills of others to his ideas. In this way, his craft developed from unmanageable monsters to the sleek raiders of the First World War, and after his death to majestic craft such as the *Graf Zeppelin*.

Other craft of diverse size and appearance were flown with varying degrees of success and not a little tragedy: from the flying bicycle of the Connecticut Professor, C.E. Ritchell, to the long line of rigid airships which sprang from the intrepid Count Ferdinand von Zeppelin. It had now become obvious to logical minds that the sinews of an Icarus are poor substitutes for the brain and cunning of a Daedalus. The paradox apparent in this ancient Greek myth is demonstrated on the one hand by technical ignorance and on the other by an Orwellian enthusiasm for invention.

The Farnborough dirigibles and the craft of E.T. Willows were among the first of Britain's airships, and were the precursors of the 216 or so airships that served in the Royal Naval Air Service as submarine scouts, patrol ships and escorts. It is interesting to note that not a single surface vessel was lost while under escort by an airship. Conversely, the history of British rigid airships was a rather chequered affair. The first rigid ship, the *Mayfly*, broke its back before it had a chance to show its paces in free flight, and, excepting a few rigids, the airships which led to the *R38* reflected the progress of lighter-than-air technology. *R80*, regarded as a good ship, only flew a total of 73 hours before she was dismantled in 1925 as part of a government economy measure.

Lord Thompson, Secretary of State for Air in 1930, pronounced that the *R101* was "... as safe as a house, except for the millionth chance." The odds, however, were not in favour of the vessel for on 5 October, the craft crashed into a hill near Beauvais in France, and Lord Thompson and forty-seven others perished in the fire that ensued. This tragedy proved disastrous to British hopes of competing with the Germans in long-distance airship travel.

Though no divine geometry, the geodetic form of construction developed and employed by Barnes Wallis on the highly successful *R100* proved that here was a designer who knew how to use materials with precision and harness the power created by the co-ordination of these materials. The *R100* made a record flight from Cardington to Montreal and back, proving the reliability of the ship. The loss of the *R101* was, however, a disincentive to the plan to link the countries of the Empire by luxury airship, and so the politicians made sure that rigid airships were excluded from Britain's transport systems. As for the *R100*, she ended her life ignominiously as £450 worth of scrap — hardly a fitting tribute to all the hard work and perseverance contributed by the best brains in aeronautics at the time.

The history of American airships is inextriciably linked with the name of The Goodyear Tyre and Rubber Company, for this firm has built most of the airships flown in America, including the greater part of that country's military craft. Although the majority of Goodyear airships were of the non-rigid type, two rigid ships were produced. The Goodyear-Zeppelin Corporation was formed to build these airships on contract to the U.S. Government. The first ship to be built was the *Akron*, commissioned in U.S. Navy service in 1931, and her sister ship, the *Macon*, commissioned in 1933. These ships were intended as aircraft carriers and constituted America's first multi-million-dollar weapon systems, but while being remarkable creations of twentieth-century technology they were superseded, untried in war, by the faster and less vulnerable aeroplane. The destruction of the *Akron* and *Macon* may be said to indicate the failure of a whole technology, but while this is in a sense true it is a superficial judgement, for it could be claimed that it was the bureaucrats who failed the new technology. Whatever other arguments pertain at least one thing is certain, that two prototype aircraft were pushed beyond the limits of their endurance in order to satisfy a somewhat reactionary anti-airship element that the *Akron* and *Macon* were useful naval craft. This attitude resulted in the tragic loss of both ships and an end to hopes for a U.S. rigid airships programme. Government involvement, however, ceased in 1940 when, after a number of plans had been studied, the final curtain was rung down on rigid airships.

World War II had already begun when the U.S. Navy finally washed its hands of rigid airships, and, when Japanese belligerency at Pearl Harbor forced America to take up arms, only a handful of non-rigid airships were in existence. Therefore, it is quite remarkable that production was stepped up so rapidly by Goodyear, that by 1943 over one hundred ships were in operation, and by the end of the war the fleet was expanded to over 165 ships. These non-rigid ships were used successfully as anti-submarine patrol craft, and operated as escorts off the East and West Coasts of America. They were even operated in places as far apart as the Mediterranean, from Gibraltar, and the Brazilian littoral.

After the war, the U.S. Navy operated a force of non-rigid airships mainly for surveillance duties, such as long distance ASW patrol, and as Early Warning Radar ships. The ZPG 2W and ZPG 3W ships carried out the latter function until the naval airship service was disbanded in the early sixties, when it was superseded by more advanced Early Warning systems. However, non-rigid ships have continued to be operated by Goodyear as aerial public relations and advertising craft, and in 1974 the *Columbia III* was replaced by an identical craft, the *Columbia IV*, the 301st airship to be built by Goodyear.

Non-rigid airships have many uses other than as public relations craft. For example, the Goodyear blimps have been used for scientific research using a variety of delicate sensing equipment, and the WDL airship bought by the Orient Lease Line is at present in use as an oceanographic research vessel. The stability offered by a lighter-than-air air platform also suits the needs of television and still camera work, and on a more sophisticated level, the photogrammetric tasks carried out by the Goodyear ships.

Goodyear believe that even in the present climate of supersonic transport, a need still exists for rigid and non-rigid airships to serve as airborne platforms, cargo and passenger carriers and for a variety of military puposes. The present Goodyear proposal is for a test-bed version of the ZPG 3W airship with a high-strength envelope made from a new fabric developed by Goodyear. This craft, costing between £10.5 and £12.5 million, would be used to evaluate the numerous applications proposed for much larger vehicles. It is hoped that this project will be financed by the U.S. Government.

The next step in the proposal, which was part of a modern airship study recently conducted for the U.S. National Aeronautics and Space Administration, represents the construction of three large ships of which the first (1) is to be a short haul, vertical take-off and landing, passenger and cargo rigid airship; the second (2) craft to be a short haul, heavy-lifter for outsize military and commercial loads; and the third (3) craft to be a 'conventional' long-range rigid airship to be used as a heavy-lifter, and unlike the other craft to obtain its total lift from helium, rather than from aerodynamics. Some details of these projects are given below.

The Goodyear study also recommended the use of small airships as passenger and cargo carriers between U.S. airports, and if acted upon, the Goodyear proposals could revolutionise air transport in America, possibly helping to reduce the internal consumption of fossil fuel and providing other benefits such as a lower atmospheric and noise pollution ratio to flights than heaver-than-air machines.

A number of other projects are being pursued by cost-conscious businessmen and well-informed technologists on both sides of the Iron Curtain. The most serious projects, those not utilised by

Project	**1**
Gross weight	40,000 lb
Static lift/gross weight	0.2*
Gross lift	—
Useful load	22,500 lb
Total volume (cu.ft.)	49,000
Gas volume (cu.ft. He)	—
Length	190 ft
Diameter	—
Fineness ratio	4.7
Width	—
Propulsion	Four tilting turboprops (8,000 h.p.)
Endurance	—
Cruise speed	100 to 150 knots
Maximum speed	—

2	3
1,510,000 lb	1,000 tons
830,000 lb	—
1,510,000 lb	—
500,000 lb (223 tons)	390 tons (at 5,000 ft)
15,750,000	39,800,000
13,400,000	—
710 ft	1,656 ft
185 ft	—
—	7.6
337 ft (with rotors)	—
Ten CH-53E helicopters	Fourteen primary turboprops and two 'loiter' turboprops
Five hours	720 hours in a 20-knot head wind
50 to 100 knots	—
—	150 knots

commercial concerns or governments seeking sensational publicity, are mentioned below.

Aérospatiale, the British Aircraft Corporation's partner in Concorde, have carried out design studies. In Britain, Skyships is working on a symmetrical lenticular rigid airship, and another British company, Airfloat Transport, on the design of a heavy-lift airship and a lighter-than-air cross-channel ferry. A third British company, Aerospace Developments, have carried out work for Shell on an airborne natural gas carrier, and are at present engaged in consultation with the U.S. Navy and the governments of Venezuela and Argentina. It is also known that feasibility studies have been carried out in Japan, West Germany and the Soviet Union.

The revival of interest in airships is considerable, and the evidence suggests that with the use of synthetic materials, developed in recent times, and the aid of modern technology for the construction of the ships and for provision of reliable instrumentation, airships, radically different from their forebears and much safer, will once again ply aerial trade routes. Safety is definitively ensured by helium, a completely inert gas seven times lighter than air, non-toxic, non-flammable and obtained economically from natural gas resources. Helium would provide the new airships with the buoyancy previously supplied by hydrogen, which the *R101* and *Hindenburg* disasters

**That is, twenty per cent of the lift would come from buoyancy and the rest from body aerodynamics in flight, or from propellers for vertical take-off.*

proved to be a highly volatile element. Hydrogen is the lightest substance known and is explosive when mixed with air, while helium, being inert, is safe but more expensive.

This book does not in any way pretend to be a detailed history of airships. Such a study would require greater space than is provided here and is in any case not within the scope of the authors' intentions. However, what has been presented here is a detailed check-list of every type and class of airship ever built. This check-list takes the form of a series of tables in which the basic data relating to each craft or class, where known, is given. In this way it is hoped that chronological comparisons can be made, and that a clear picture of the development of design and motive power, the use of materials, and the levels of success obtained can be referred to with ease. Background information is given, on the most important aspects of airship development, in the cameos that accompany each sequence of tables. However, for information on the earliest pioneering attempts, the reader is referred to the first half of the introduction. Additional information has been included in the captions accompanying the photographs.

Eugène **Miroslaw Koleśnik**

Acknowledgements

The authors have received valuable help from many individuals and organisations during the preparation of this book, but in particular would like to thank the following for providing photographs and information; Brian J. Beesley and Thomas B. Riley of Goodyear; Denis H.R. Archer; Ronald T. Pretty; John W.R. Taylor; Rex King; J. White of Short Brothers & Harland; Mr. Stott of R.A.E. Farnborough; the staff of R.A.E. Cardington; the photographic department of Vickers; Norman Polmar; William McE Miller, Jr. of Aereon Corp.; Andrew Halushka of the Tucker Airship Co.; Larry J. Manderscheid of Raven Industries; Brian J. Bowland; the Imperial War Museum; Paul Stumpf; Howard Levy; Brecht Brugger; Topical Press; Novosti Press; Keystone Press and the photographic department of the U.S. Navy.

We are grateful to William Heinemann Ltd. for permission to quote from *Slide Rule* by Nevil Shute.

Thanks are due to Kate Spells for translating original French and Italian documents, to Alex Vanags for translating early Russian material, and to Hazel Pattinson and Lorraine Gamman for typing the bulk of the book, and also to Isobel Smythe-Wood for reading the proofs. Last but not least we owe a debt beyond measure to the publishers, Macdonald & Jane's Ltd., and in particular to Stuart Bannerman and Megan Turner of Jane's production department for their unfailing patience and sound advice.

AUSTRIA

The Hänlein Airship

Paul Hänlein's airship was 84,880 cubic feet in capacity, and the craft was powered by a gas engine which drove a single slow turning tractor-type propeller. The results obtained with this ship were disappointing and she was dismantled.

The Hänlein semi-rigid airship of 1872

Boemches 1. This Austrian ship was not successful and was deleted in 1913

M1, the first Austrian Army airship. This Parseval ship was trimmed by use of her two ballonets

AUSTRIAN MILITARY AND PRIVATE AIRSHIPS

Class/Name	Make/Type	Launched	Vol. (cu.ft.)	Dimensions (ft) Length	Diam.	Engines No.(hp each)	Speed max. mph	Remarks
Austria	SM (NR)	1911(?)	289,960	30.3	45.5	2(100-130)	38.03	A vertical take-off and landing craft.
Boemcher I and II	Boemcher (NR)	1912	97,130	188	29.7	2 Körting (36)	24.5	Not successful and deleted in 1913.
Estaric	Renner and Gratz (NR)	1909	24,170	105.6	(width 19.8)	1 Puch (40)	21.5	Wrecked in a storm while landing in 1910.
Hänlein	Hänlein (NR)	1872	84,720	165	(width 30.3)	1 Lenoir (coal gas) (3)	11.8	Dismantled as the engine was unable to drive the ship.
Hildebrandt	— (NR)	—	85,000	164	30	1 Lenoir (coal gas) (11)	—	—
M1 (Parseval. PL4)	MLG (NR)	1909	86,485	165	28.2	1 Austro Daimler (75)	27.92	First Austrian Army airship. Built by Motor-Luftfahrzeug.
M2 (Lebaudy)	MLG (SR)	1910	169,536	231	(width 35.9)	1 Austro Daimler (130)	27.8	Constructed in Vienna to a Lebaudy design.
M3	Körting (NR)	1911	127,152	244.4	34.6	2 Körting (75)	30.5	Destroyed when in collision with an aeroplane near Vienna 20.6.14.
Mannsbarth	Stagl Mannsbarth (NR)	1911	289,600	—	—	2 (150)	40	Parseval type.

The rear car of the *Austria*, showing the rudder and one of her propellers

Mannsbarth's *Austria* of 1911

BELGIUM

Belgique I	Louis Goddard (SR)	1909	95,364	160.8	32.1	2 Vivinus (50)	23	Made 23 flights before being deflated in 1909.
Belgique II	Goddard and Germain (SR)	1910	141,280	214.5	36.3	1 main (120)	26.5	Reconstructed *No.I.*
Belgique III	Goddard and Germain (SR)	1910(?)	141,280	214.5	36.3	2 Germain (60)	32.5	Reconstructed *No.II.* Presented in 1910 to the Belgian Government by the King of the Belgians. Scrapped 1914 (?).
Lambert	Zodiac type (NR)	1910(?)	—	—	—	—	—	Sold to a private concern in the U.S.A.

La Belgique 1, built in France by Louis Godard for Robert Goldschmidt, made her first flight on 28 June 1909 near Brussels

THE NETHERLANDS

Duindight	Zodiac (NR)	1911	32,000	114	22.5	1 Daimler (30)	26.7	This small edition of *Zodiac III* was presented to the Dutch Army in 1911 by M. Jachens.

Astra-Torres

One of the most successful French airship manufacturers was the Société Astra des Constructions Aéronautiques, a balloon manufacturing concern. The company started building airships after carrying out reconstruction work on the first Lebaudy airship. About twelve Astra-designed ships were built before the company took over and developed the envelope designed by the Spaniard, Torres Quevedo.

The airships, known as the Astra-Torres type, had an envelope arranged in the form of a trefoil instead of being circular. Three fabric curtains maintained the shape of the envelope, and were perforated in order not to divide the gas space into three separate compartments. The ridge formed by the junction of the two lower lobes was connected by internal rigging to the upper ridges, and the suspension system of the car was attached to the outside of the lower ridge. Thus the rigging for the distribution of the main load over the envelope was enclosed inside the envelope, with a consequent reduction in resistance. This shortening of the rigging enabled the car to be slung nearer the envelope than was otherwise possible. Astra *XIV*, *XVII* and *XIX* were bought by the British Navy, and this type of rigging was then subsequently employed in the British Coastal and C Star airships.

After the failure of the Astra Grand Cruiser *Pilatre de Rozier*, two smaller ships were made from her parts. These ships, the *Alsace* and *Pilatre de Rozier II*, were used by the French Army. From 1916 until 1922 the Astra company built a series of excellent airships for the French Navy.

Adjudant Reau landing at Verdun

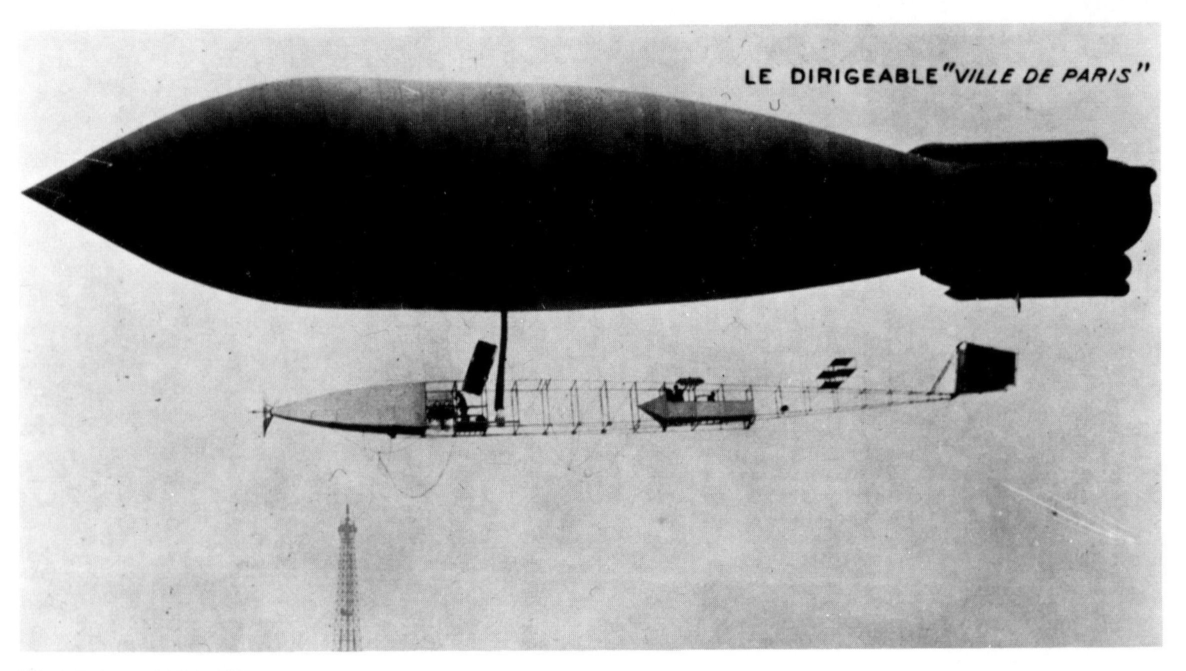

Ville de Paris over Paris in 1906

The "Grand Cruiser" *Pilatre de Rozier*

AT1 was the first successful Astra ship in which the Torres Quevedo suspension system was employed

L'Alsace taking off from Issy-le-Moulineaux

The ASW ship *AT 18*

The car, planes and propellers of the *Conté*

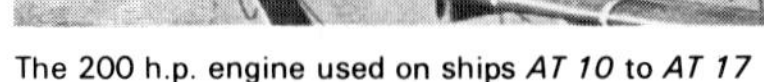

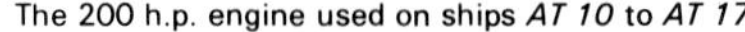

The 200 h.p. engine used on ships *AT 10* to *AT 17*

The fore part of the car used on ships *AT 5* to *AT 9*

Chalais-Meudon

The French State Airship Factory at Chalais-Meudon operated from the 1880s until 1940. A total of eleven airships were built by this factory for the French Army and the French Navy. Although only *Fleurus I* saw service with the army during the war, the C-M ships proved to be most valuable when employed with the Navy on patrol and anti-submarine duties. The larger of these ships were later used on convoy duties. *T1*, a ship with a very high aspect ratio, which was to be stationed at Bizerta on the North African coast was lost with all hands off the coast of Sardinia in May 1917. Her successor, the *T2*, *Captain Caussin*, a ship with a lower aspect ratio, was much larger and had more horse-power at her disposal. *CM1* to *4* were regarded as excellent airships. The last four Chalais-Meudon airships were, with the exception of *CM5*, never completed. *CM5* was sold to the Americans, indicating that these craft were regarded as a successful class of airships.

Fleurus 1 at St Cyr in 1912

A bow view of *La France*

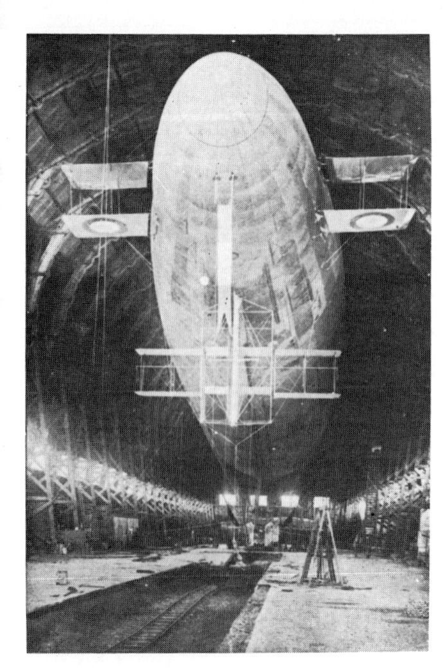

A stern view of *Fleurus III*

The enclosed streamlined car of *T 1*

The shaft drive and propeller used on ships *CM 1* to *CM 4*

Adjudant Vincenot with a shortened car, and the control surfaces and planes fixed to the envelope

Clément-Bayard

The airships of the Maison Clément-Bayard were mainly used for military purposes, and a few of them were very successful, making many operational flights, and standing up to severe punishment from the guns of both German and French troops. However, even though the Clément-Bayard designs were robust, none of them showed many definite advances. *CB1*, in particular, had thick inflated stabilising fins at the stern of the envelope, which added seriously to the head resistance. In the later types, these encumbrances were abandoned in favour of the more efficient plane fins.

In 1913 and 1914 *Adjutant Vincenot* and *Dupuy de Lôme* were improved by shortening their long cars and placing all fins on the envelope. *Montgolfier* was built with a short car having booms fore and aft, and an experimental lifting propeller was tried out. The last of the Clément-Bayard ships *General Meusnier*, a ship of some 810,000 cubic feet, was a failure as were all of the "Grand Cruisers" built by Astra, Clément-Bayard and Zodiac.

The elevating planes of *Adjudant Vincenot*, before modification

The control car of *Adjudant Vincenot*

Clément-Bayard VI before she was sold to Russia

General Meusnier

Lebaudy

The airships constructed by the Lebaudy brothers were popular with many European governments. It is perhaps significant that the second Lebaudy airship was taken over by the French Government. It thus secured the distinction of being the first airship considered suitable for military operations.

In the years that followed many similar, but continuously improving, airship types were constructed by the Lebaudy firm. The largest ship was in fact larger than any other non-rigid or semi-rigid built up to that time. This airship was purchased by a subscription

The car of the semi-rigid *Selle de Beauchamps*

La Jaune

organised by the *Morning Post* newspaper, and had a capacity of 353,166 cubic feet. She was almost 338 feet in length and had a diameter of 39 feet and 3 inches. Three ballonets were provided and two 135 h.p. Panhard engines, each driving a 16-foot airscrew, provided the means of locomotion. This ship was flown from the Lebaudy factory at Moisson across the Channel to Farnborough on 26 October 1910, a distance of about 230 miles. Unfortunately, the ship had a brief career, being damaged on delivery and finally wrecked on her trial flight.

By 4 May 1911 twelve Lebaudy airships were built, the last being the Grand Cruiser *Tissandier* which was not accepted by the French authorities. The six ships taken over by the French Army were used mainly for training purposes.

It is interesting to note that M. Julliot, the Lebaudy engineer, went to America in 1917 to work with the Goodrich company on "B" class airships.

The Lebaudy ship *Selle de Beauchamps*

Santos-Dumont

The enthusiasm of the Brazilian aviator, Alberto Santos-Dumont, was largely responsible for the development of the non-rigid airship. Although this gentleman was inspired by the work of early pioneers, in particular Giffard and the Tissandier brothers, he lacked the technical and scientific knowledge of Count Zeppelin's designers, but he made up for this by his wealth and dapper style. However, he was an experienced balloonist and a clever mechanic, and he learnt the rudiments of non-rigid airship design as he went along; he

Tissandier. This ship was not successful as she was too slow and did not have large enough control surfaces

apparently failed to understand the need for stabilising fins, but proved himself a clever pilot of small airships, even using them as aerial runabouts in Paris. Santos-Dumont built a total of 15 airships and succeeded in winning a prize of £30,000 for flying successfully from Saint Cloud and returning to the starting point after making a circuit of the Eiffel Tower. The length of the course was 7 miles, and Santos-Dumont succeeded in completing the course in 29½ minutes, gaining the prize which he divided among his mechanics and a number of charities. After constructing his last ship Santos-Dumont turned his attention to dynamic aircraft, in which he was also to become a pioneer.

Zodiac

The Société Zodiac, which at first was mainly occupied with balloon construction, became involved in the manufacture of airships for sporting and publicity purposes. These airships were produced from 1908 until 1936 and a number of them were exported to other countries, including Holland, Russia and South America. Non-rigid, semi-rigid and rigid airships were all produced by this company, and a number of them saw war service, a few of them being based in North Africa, and remaining in service until 1937.

Zodiac Motorised Kite-Balloons

A number of motorised kite-balloons were used by the French armed forces before the Second World War. The first of these hybrid craft was developed by the Société Zodiac for the military and was employed with success on the 1934 manoeuvres.

The motorised kite-balloon consisted of a normal kite-balloon envelope to which was attached a self-contained car carrying an

Santos-Dumont's first ship making her first flight on 18 September 1898

Santos-Dumont No. 4 in 1900

Santos-Dumont No. 5 before making a forced landing on the roof of a Paris hotel

engine and the control surfaces. This unit was slung under the kite-balloon, using a rope suspension frame. It was claimed that, using a standard car, a kite-balloon could be converted to the motorised variety in six to nine minutes.

The Zodiac *Moto-ballon*, as the motorised kit-balloon was called, had a 60 h.p. Salmson engine in its detachable wooden monocoque nacelle, an elevator plane forward and a rudder aft. A skid chassis protected the airscrew, but a detachable wheel chassis was provided for road transport. A crew of two could be carried in the cockpit.

Sufficient fuel was carried for two hours flying at 40 m.p.h.

Three types of motorised kite-balloon were developed by the Société Zodiac, MBZ 1, 2 and 3. MBZ 3 balloons were used at the Front until 1940, mainly for "night work". Twenty-four *Moto-ballons* were supplied to the Armée de L'air. One of these balloons was used after the war for publicity purposes.

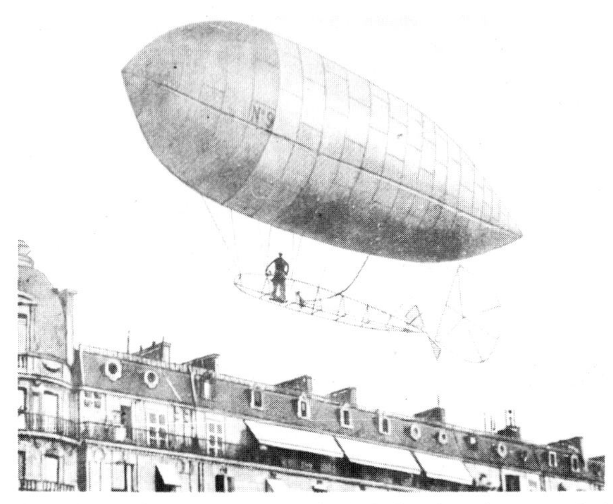

Santos-Dumont No. 6 was used as a runabout in Paris and was often seen parked outside restaurants and the apartment of Santos-Dumont

Zodiac 1 making its first flight as *Le Petit Journal* on 29 November 1909

The car of *D'Arlandes*

Commandant Coutelle at Verdun in 1915

Champagne at Toul in 1916

V12, the last Zodiac airship to be constructed

The Zodiac Moto-ballon *MBZ 3*

Spiess the Zodiac airship which had a rigid wooden framework

VZ 16. Ships of this class were larger editions of the "VZI" class

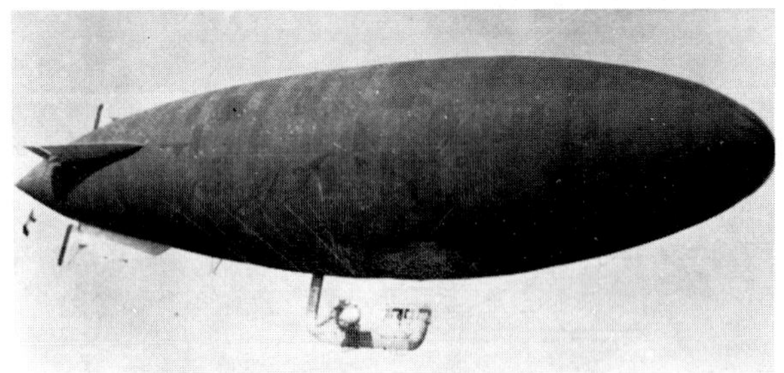

The Zodiac non-rigid *VZ 6*

ZD5.

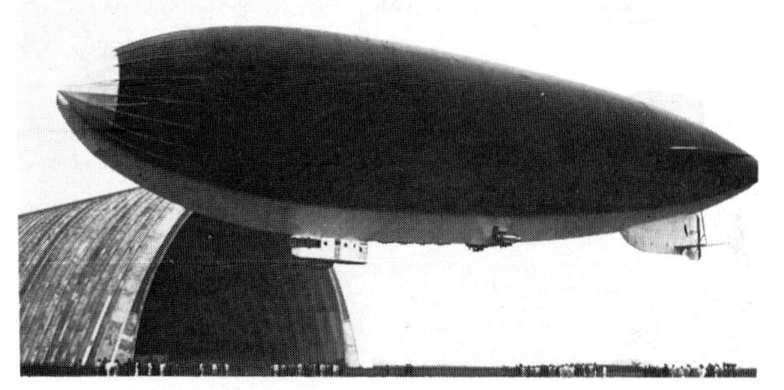

The Zodiac semi-rigid airship *E 9*

FRENCH AIRSHIPS

Class/Name	Make/Type	Launched	Vol. (cu.ft.)	Dimensions (ft) Length	Diam.	Engines No.(hp each)	Speed max. mph	Remarks
Ville de Paris	Astra (NR)	1907	114,757 (113,024?)	196.10 (207.9?)	34.6	1 Chenu (60)	22.3	Commissioned from the Surcouf Workshops by M. Henry Deutsch de la Meurthe. Presented to the French Army and used as a replacement for the *Patrie*. Stationed at Verdun.
Ville de Paris (enlarged)	Astra (NR)	1908	187,116 (134,140?)	117.8	—	1 Chenu (80)	27.2	
Ville de Bordeaux **and Ville de Nancy**	Astra (NR)	1908-09	118,255	184.8	33	1 Chenu or Clément-Bayard (50)	—	Passenger carrying ships. Names changed according to towns visited. Also known as *Transaeriene I* and *II*. The latter ship was much larger.
Ville de Pau and Ville de Lucerne (Transaerien I and II)	Astra (NR)	1909	157,967	198	40.26	1 Clément-Bayard (90)	—	
Espana	Astra (NR)	1909	148,260	214.5	36.6	1 Panhard Levassor (110)	—	Sold to Spain.
Ville de Bruxelles	Astra (NR)	1910	292,990	249.8	47.19	2 Pipe (110)	—	All ships of this class had cruciform tail units inflated with hydrogen.
Colonel Renard (Vedette)	Astra (NR)	1909	148,260	214.5	36.63	1 Panhard Levassor (110)	30	Built for Verdun Army Station.
Adjudant Réau (Cruiser)	Astra (NR)	1911	315,935	286.3	46.2	2 Braisier (110)	32	Last flight made 8.8.1914 at Issy.
A.T.1 (Vedette)	Astra-Torres (NR)	1911	56,496	157	27.7	1 Chenu (50)	32.3	Experimental craft. First really successful Torres Quevedo ship.
Lt. Chauré (Cruiser)	Astra (NR)	1913	312,493	276.5	46.2	2 Panhard (110)	32	Similar to *Adjudent Réau*. Not used in WWI.
Conté (Scout)	Astra (NR)	1912	234,745	214.5	46.2	2 Chenu (80)	40	Shot down and repaired twice.
Astra XIII	Astra (NR)	1913	370,755	255.11	47.5	2 Chenu (200)	—	The last of the traditional large-car Astra ships. Sold to Russian Army in 1913.

Class/Name	Make/Type	Launched	Vol. (cu.ft.)	Dimensions (ft) Length	Diam.	Engines No.(hp each)	Speed max. mph	Remarks
Pilatre de Rozier (Grand Cruiser)	Astra-Torres (NR)	1915	812,130	426.5	54	4 Chenu (250)	52.8	As pressure could not be maintained it was decided to build two ships from her parts.
Alsace and Pilatre de Rozier	Astra-Torres (NR)	1915-16	494,340	295	54	2 Chenu (250)	37.2 and 42	Sister ships built from parts of the dismantled "Grand Cruiser". Both destroyed in WWI.
La Flandre	Astra-Torres (NR)	1917	570,256	—	—	4 Renault (250)	58	Deleteu after five flights.
AT 1-4	Astra-Torres (NR)	1916	229,515	223.1	44.5	2 Renault (150)	50	First French Navy airships.
AT 5-9	Astra-Torres (NR)	1917	268,356	232.11	48.6	2 Renault (150)	48	Width: 52.6ft. Height: 65.7ft.
AT 10-17	Astra-Torres (NR)	1918	293,073	246.1	48.6	2 Renault or Hispano Suiza (200)	49	Built to carry a 75mm cannon in addition to bombs.
AT 18-19	Astra-Torres (NR)	1919	377,817	262.6	52.6	2 Renault (250)	52.8	Carried heavy ASW weapons.
AT 24	Astra-Torres (NR)	1920	402,534	269	59	2 Maybach (260)	52.8	Believed to have been sold to Japan.
E6	Reconstructed Astra-Torres (NR)	1936(?)	353,000	246.1	—	2 Hispano Suiza (300-350)	40+	Reconstructed AT. Used for training at Rochfort.
La France	Chalais-Meudon (NR)	1884	65,817	165.3	27.5	1 Gramme Electric (8 then 9)	12	First airship to make a circular flight. Last flight made 22.9.85.
Fleurus I (Scout)	Chalais-Meudon (NR)	1912	229,515	252.7	41	2 Clément-Bayard (80)	37.2	Bombed in shed in 1918.
Fleurus II and III/ Lorrain and Tunisie	Chalais-Meudon (NR)	1915-16	370,755	305	45.11	2 Clément-Bayard (220)	43.4	Deleted after Armistice in 1918.
T1	Chalais-Meudon (NR)	1915	197,736	272.4	35.7	2 Salmson (160)	62	Lost with crew in 1916.
T2/Captain Caussin	Chalais-Meudon (NR)	1917	322,027	272.4	45.11	2 Salmson (240)	54	Employed by U.S. Navy in 1918.
CM1-4	Chalais-Meudon (NR)	1917-18	194,205	229.8	37.6	2 Salmson (150)	49.7	French Naval airships based in the Western approaches. These ships carried a crew of five.

FRENCH AIRSHIPS

Class/Name	Make/Type	Launched	Vol. (cu.ft.)	Dimensions (ft) Length	Diam.	Engines No.(hp each)	Speed max. mph	Remarks
CM 5-8	Chalais-Meudon (NR)	1919	321,321	265.9	45	2 Salmson (250)	49.7	Designed to carry heavy armament. *CM5* was the only ship of the class completed by the end of the war. She was subsequently sold to the U.S.A.
Clément-Bayard I	Clément-Bayard (NR) Envelope by Astra	1908	123,585	184.8	33	1 C-B (116)	29.8	Bought by the Russian Army. Lost on trials in 1909.
Clément-Bayard II	Clément-Bayard (NR)	1910	22,450	54	43	2C-B (125)	—	This was the first airship to cross from the Continent to Britain.
Clément-Bayard III/ Adjudant Vincenot	Clément-Bayard (NR)	1911	317,850	287	44.2	2 C-B (120)	30-32	Modified in 1913 together with *Dupuy-de-Lôme*. The car was shortened and planes were put on the envelope.
Clément-Bayard IV/ Dupuy-de-Lôme	Clément-Bayard (NR)	1912	346,000	287	44.2	2 C-B (125)	30	Shot down and wrecked by French troops in mistake for a Zeppelin on 24 August 1914.
Montgolfier/CB V Scout	Clément-Bayard (NR)	1913	234,811	237	40	2 C-B (70)	36	She originally had a lifting propeller, but this was too small and placed too near the envelope to be effective, and so was removed in 1914.
CB VI	Clément-Bayard (NR)	1913-14	346,038	287	44.28	2 C-B (120)	32-33	Sold to Russia.
General Meusnier (Grand Cruiser)	Clément-Bayard NR)	1915	812,130	526	52.6	4 C-B (250)	46.6	An enlarged *Montgolfier*. Made three flights.
Ex-General Meusnier	Clément-Bayard (NR)	1916	812,130	526	52.6	4 C-B (250)	46.6	A long car was substituted for the original short car and booms. The engines were

Class/Name	Make/Type	Launched	Vol. (cu.ft.)	Dimensions (ft) Length	Diam.	Engines No.(hp each)	Speed max. mph	Remarks
								fitted at the extreme ends of the car. The ballonets were placed close to the ends of the envelope. This was the last Clément-Bayard ship. She was sold to Russia.
Faure	Jacques Faure (NR)	1909	36,553	108	24	1 Buchet (28)	20	Flown inflated with coal gas.
Lebaudy I/Le Jaune	Lebaudy (SR)	1902	64,800	173	30	1 Daimler (35-40)	21.7	New envelope and motor fitted in 1903.
Lebaudy II (enlarged)	Lebaudy (SR)	1904	94,000	190	—	1 Daimler (40)	—	Made twelve ascents.
Lebaudy III	Lebaudy (SR)	1905	105,000	—	—	1 Daimler-Mercedes (50)	24.8	Enlarged to 116,623 cu.ft., and had elevating planes fitted. Army school ship. Deleted 1910.
Lebaudy 4/Patrie	Lebaudy (SR)	1906	113,250	199	33.9	1 Panhard (60)	27.9	Carried out to sea by a stray wind and lost in 1907.
Lebaudy 5/République	Lebaudy (SR)	1908	130,647	200.2	36	1 Panhard (70)	31	The first French airship to be used on manoeuvres. Broken propeller flew into envelope which burst killing the crew.
Lebaudy 6/Russie	Lebaudy (SR)	1909	128,000	203.5	36	1 Panhard (70)	30.4	Sold to Russian in 1909.
Lebaudy 7/Liberté	Lebaudy (SR)	1909	162,425	213.3	41	1 Panhard (120)	27.9	Had stronger envelope than former Lebaudy ships. Modified and given two motors.
Lebaudy 8/M2	Lebaudy (SR)	1910	169,536	231	36.1	1 Austro Daimler (130)	27.8	Built in Vienna to Lebaudy design for Austrian Army.
Lebaudy 9/Morning Post	Lebaudy (SR)	1910	353,166	337.75	39.3	2 Panhard (135)	36	Sold to Great Britain. Wrecked flying low in 1911.
Lebaudy/Kretchet	Lebaudy (SR)	1911	201,195	229.8	45.11	2 Panhard (100)	31	Built in Russia to Lebaudy design for Russian Army.

FRENCH AIRSHIPS

Class/Name	Make/Type	Launched	Vol. (cu.ft.)	Dimensions (ft) Length	Diam.	Engines No.(hp each)	Speed max. mph	Remarks
Lebaudy 10/Captain Marschal	Lebaudy (SR)	1911	254,232	278.10	42	2 Panhard (80)	31	Training ship.
Lebaudy 11/Selle de Beauchamps	Lebaudy (SR)	1911	353,100	292	47.9	2 Panhard (70)	27	Took part in 1911 manoeuvres.
Lebaudy 12/Tissandier	Lebaudy (NR)	1914	741,510	426.6	54.2	7 Salmson (120)	37.2	"Grand Cruiser", refused by French Army, and later by British Navy.
Malécot	La Chambre-Malécot (SR)	1907	37,227	108.9	24.09	1 Buchet (30)	24	Hybrid H/A and L/A ship. Deflated and her parts were used in other craft.
Marcay	Experimental (NR)	1909	12,000	100	12.6	—	8	An experimental ship with a lift of 1,852 lb.
Bradsky	Bradsky-La Chambre (NR)	1902	30,005	112.7	19.8	1 Buchet (16)	—	The car became detached from the envelope and Baron Bradsky and his crew were killed. Accident caused by faulty suspension.
Pax	Severo-La Chambre (SR)	1902	70,600	99	15.6	1 Buchet (12)	—	Exploded killing Severo and his companion.
Santos Dumont 1	SD, La Chambre (NR)	1898	6,354	82.5	11.5	1 De Dion Beuton (3)	17.90(?)	Two unsuccessful ascents.
Santos Dumont 2	Santos Dumont, La Chambre (NR)	1899	7,062	82.5	12.54	1 De Dion Beuton (3½)	—	Gross lift 480lb. One unsuccessful ascent made as pressure could not be kept up. Crashed.
Santos Dumont 3	SD, La Chambre (NR)	1899(?)	17,650	65.7	24.6	1 De Dion Beuton (3½)	15	Inflated with coal gas. First successful Santos Dumont ship.
Santos Dumont 4	SD, La Chambre (NR)	1900(?)	14,825	129	17	1 Buchet (7)	—	Gross lift 1,000lb. Envelope enlarged and used for *Santos Dumont 5*.
Santos Dumont 5	SD, La Chambre (NR)	1901(?)	21,900 (19,415?)	109	17	1 Buchet (12)	18(?)	"Landed" on roof of Paris hotel after a number of

Class/Name	Make/Type	Launched	Vol. (cu.ft.)	Dimensions (ft) Length	Diam.	Engines No.(hp each)	Speed max. mph	Remarks
								flights and was never flown again.
Santos Dumont 6	SD, La Chambre (NR)	1901	22,239	108.9	19.8	1 Buchet (12)	—	Circled the Eiffel Tower.
Santos Dumont 7	SD, La Chambre (NR)	—	44,372	165	26.4	1 Clément-Bayard (60)	—	A racing ship sent to the U.S.A. Sabotaged in St. Louis.
Santos Dumont 8	SD, La Chambre (NR)	1913	7,770	45.10	16.6	Clément-Bayard (3)	12	Only one ascent made.
Santos Dumont 9	SD, La Chambre (NR)	1903	7,770	45.10	18.15	1 Clément-Bayard (3)	12-15	Very successful ship. Known as *Baladeuse*.
Santos Dumont 10	SD, La Chambre (NR)	1903	70,953	157	27.9	1 (20)	—	Intended to carry passengers but never flown as such.
Santos Dumont 11	SD, La Chambre (NR)	—	42,384	112.2	33.6	1 Buchet (16)	—	Not completed.
Santos Dumont 13	SD, La Chambre (NR)	1904	67,108	—	—	None	—	Not fitted with an engine. Used for experiments in static climbing.
Santos Dumont 14	SD, La Chambre (NR)	—	6,570	134	11.1	1 Buchet (15)	—	Only one ascent. Not successful.
Santos Dumont 15	SD, La Chambre (NR)	—	6,570	134	11.1	None	—	Used in connection with first aeroplane experiment.
Santos Dumont 16	SD, La Chambre (NR)	1907	—	—	—	Antoinette	—	Stranded on a tree after her first flight.
Tissandier	Tissandier (NR)	1888	37,100	91.8	49.8	1 Siemans Electric (?)	—	Second flight made Sept. 26 1889 but proved too slow. Deleted.
La Vaulx	La Vaulx-Mallet (NR)	1906	25,769	107.2	21.2	1 Ader (14)	—	Unstable. Later given rudder and horizontal fins mounted on the stern of the boom.
Zodiac I/Le Petit Journal	Zodiac (NR)	1909	24,717	98.5	23	1 Clerget (16)	16.1	Could be flown on coal gas.
Zodiac II/Le Petit Journal	Zodiac (NR)	—	28,248	106	23.5	1 Clerget (16)	16.1	Carried a crew of one, inflated with coal gas and a crew of two with hydrogen.

FRENCH AIRSHIPS.

Class/Name	Make/Type	Launched	Vol. (cu.ft.)	Dimensions (ft) Length	Diam.	Engines No.(hp each)	Speed max. mph	Remarks
Zodiac III	Zodiac (NR)	1909	49,434	134	27.95	1 Ballot (45)	27.9	Exhibition ship. Piloted by Count de la Vaulx.
Zodiac V	Zodiac (NR)	1910	31,779	106	—	1 (45)	18.6	Sold to American millionaire, Mr Davis, who took the ship to the U.S.A.
Zodiac VI	Zodiac (NR)	1910	49,434	134	27.95	1 Mercedes (30)	—	Built for Belgian Army as a training ship. Enlarged to 60,027cu.ft. in 1913.
Zodiac VI/Duindight	Zodiac (NR)	1911	32,000	114	22.15	1 Daimler (30)	26.7	Gross lift 1,176lb. Presented to the Dutch Army in 1911 by M Jachens. Deleted about 1914.
Zodiac VIII and IX/ Tchäika and Korchoune	(7 and 8?) (NR)	1910	75,000	157.6	32.10	1 DG (60)	24.8	Sold to the Russian Army and tested in Russia by Count de la Vaulx.
Zodiac X (IX?)/ Le Temps	Zodiac (NR)	1911	81,213	165	29.6	1 DG (110)	31	*Vedette*, used as school ship at St. Cyr.
Zodiac XI/Captain Ferber	Zodiac (NR)	1911	211,860	249.4	42.6	2 Dansette Gillet (100)	34.7	Scout, deleted 1914.
Zodiac/Spiess (Z12?)	Zodiac (R)	1913	451,968	370	44.5	2 Chenu (200)	—	Built of wood and when
Zodiac/Spiess (Z12?)	Above enlarged (R)	—	579,084	459	44.5	2 Chenu (200)	—	enlarged had insufficient lift. Deleted 1914.
Zodiac/Commandant Coutelle (Z13?)	Zodiac (NR)	1913	335,445	301.10	45.11	2 Dansette Gillet (200)	38.5	Based at Epinol. Enlarged to increase lift 1914.
Zodiac/Commandant Coutelle (Z13?)	Above enlarged (NR)	1915	423,720	297	—	—	—	Altitude: 8,200 ft. Destroyed while on raid. Crew safe.
D'Arlandes and Champagne (Z14?)	Zodiac (NR)	1915/16	501,402	301.2	52.6	2 Zodiac (220)	42	Both built from the parts of a Grand Cruiser which never flew. Taken over by the Navy.
VZ 1-5 (+ 1)	Zodiac (NR)	1916	97,102	155.8	35.6	2 Renault (80)	47.8	ASW ships. Six in Class. The first ship of this class was made from parts imported from Belgium.

Class/Name	Make/Type	Launched	Vol. (cu.ft.)	Dimensions (ft)		Engines No.(hp each)	Speed max. mph	Remarks
				Length	Diam.			
VZ 7-15	Zodiac (NR)	1918	98,840	155.8	—	2 Renault (80)	47.8	Approx. width: 40.4ft; Weight: 55.9lb.
VZ 16-23	Zodiac (NR)	1919	109,461	157.6	36.1	2 Hispano (150)	50	Larger edition of *VZ1* class. *VZ17-21* not built.
ZD 1-5	Zodiac (NR)	1918	218,922	236.3	42.8	2 Hispano Suiza (200)	49.7	Height: 65.7. Crew of five.
ZD US/ZD 6-8	Zodiac (NR)	1919	326,500	264	49.5	2 Renault (250)	49	Only *ZD6* built. Sold to U.S. Navy.
Vedette L'Ecole	Zodiac (NR)	1920	42,000	118	26.4	1 Anzani (70)	43	Charles Dolfus helped to design this ship.
VZ6/V6	Zodiac (NR)	1923	141,200	148.5	—	2 Hispano Suiza (150)	40.92	Built for French Navy.
VZ7/V7	Zodiac (NR)	1926	123,550	190.6	58.1	2 Hispano Suiza (150)	42.1	Built for French Navy.
V10	Zodiac (SR)	1924	119,000	151	42.7	2 Salmson (120)	62	Valves opening at high speed caused it to crash in 1930.
E8 and E9	Zodiac (SR)	1931/33	353,200	264	56.1	2 Hispano Suiza (350)	63.8	*E9* crashed due to valve trouble.
V11	Zodiac (NR)	1931	120,889	148.5	42.9	2 Salmson (120)	60	Successful craft with trefoil (tri-lobed) envelope. Speed of 70 mph claimed. Four crew members.
V12	Zodiac (NR)	1936	141,906	161.4	28.6	2 Salmson (270)	64	The last French Naval Airship. Towed while on belly mast so reducing ground crew. Crew of four or five.
Oehmichen 1	Zodiac/Balloon-Helicopter (NR)	1921	5,085	—	—	Dutheil-Chalmers (25)	—	Useful lift 587lb.
Devil's Helistat	Zodiac (NR)	1930(?)	21,188	—	—	1 (60) and 1 (12)	—	Helicopter machine based at Toussus-le-Noble.
Hélicostat	Zodiac/Etienne Oehmichen (NR)	1931	19,400	—	—	1 Salmson (40)	—	A ship of 62,138 cu. ft built in 1931. Last ship built 1932.

The military airship *P 1* which made its first flight on 13 August 1908

GERMANY

Gross-Basenach

The Gross-Basenach airships were a series of successful semi-rigids built to the design of Major von Basenach. His first ship was a small experimental craft based on the Lebaudy design. The aim of the Major was to produce a better airship, increasing speed and range with each craft he built, but the Gross-Basenach ships were superseded by rigid Zeppelin craft by 1913. However, *M4* was employed by the German Navy until 1915.

The semi-rigid *Ersatz M IV* which could be moored or landed on water. The machine gun position can be seen on the top forward part of the envelope

The car of the military airship *P II*

The Parseval-Natz semi-rigid, *Trumpf 1*

M II, the second Gross Basenach ship

The advertising and passenger carrying ship *PN 30*

Parseval Airships

Parseval airships were made in Germany from 1906 to the designs of Major von Parseval, and, of the 27 craft built, several were supplied to other countries, including the one bought by the British navy. The first Parseval airship had two ballonets, one fore and one aft, so that its trim could be controlled by regulating the air in the two compartments. Horizontal and vertical control surfaces were attached to the stern of the envelope, and an automatic

The non-rigid *Suchard 1*

compensating system of suspension cables enabled the axis of the car to be kept horizontal, even when pitching occurred. It is worth noting here that the car suspension of all non-rigid and semi-rigid airships is so arranged that whatever the angle of pitch the car is always parallel with the envelope. The success of this airship encouraged production of larger craft embodying similar characteristics. In later Parseval airships a wind tunnel was used to determine a hull with a streamlined shape, and a system of rigging was evolved which had most of the advantages of the Astra-Torres design and few of its most serious faults. Most Parseval airships were used for military purposes, and production of these types ceased in 1917. However, three small Parseval-Natz airships were built and used successfully for publicity purposes after the First World War.

The car and starboard engines of the *Flying Musketeer*. Note the "night sign" on the envelope

Westdeutsche Luftwerbung

Herr Theodor Wüllenkemper founded the WDL airship works at Essen-Mülheim in 1969, with the objective of building a new generation of non-rigid airships.

The first three designs, *WDL 1, 2* and *3* are intended as experimental craft, increasing in size progressively and meant to explore new concepts to simplify the operation of these craft. Subject to successful development, it is planned to embody their basic constructional, control and handling concepts in a larger standard production craft, which is designated *WDL 4*.

WDL 4 is intended to explore special gondola configurations to permit the carriage of international standard freight containers. These will take the form of interchangeable passenger/cargo modules. The power plant mountings, rotatable through 360 degrees, will allow the propeller thrust to be used not only for fore and aft propulsion, but also in vertical modes to enhance lift or assist in landing procedures.

The Standard *WDL 4* airship will have a gross volume of 2,260,140 cubic feet, and a payload of 66,140 lb. It is expected that this ship will have a heating system, from the exhaust, to raise the temperature of the helium lifting gas.

WDL 1 (Serial No. 100)

Construction of *WDL 1* was completed in mid-1972 and the first flight, piloted by Konrad Hess, was made on 12 August 1972. This airship, named *The Flying Musketeer*, was severely damaged during a storm on 13 November 1972, was repaired during the subsequent winter months and began flying again on 28 April 1973. At this time the airship was renamed *Wicküler*.

The envelope is made of synthetic fabric and is helium-filled. An automatic pressure control system has been developed to maintain effective control of pressure during flight as well as on the ground, to preserve the shape and stability of the craft at all times. On each side of the envelope there is a panel 131 feet 3 inches by 26 feet 3 inches, together these carry 10,000 electric light bulbs for advertising displays.

The power plant consists of 2 Rolls Royce Continental aero-engines, and all the fuel for these engines is contained in cells mounted within the envelope. This arrangement provides maximum capacity in the gondola.

WDL 1 (Serial No. 101)

This craft was completed in the late summer of 1972 and made a first flight during October. The envelope was damaged when the airship's inflatable hangar collapsed during a storm in November of that year, but before this she survived winds gusting at over 100 m.p.h. After repairs the ship was taken to Japan, where she is operated by Orient Lease Co. Ltd. of Tokyo. German and American airship pilots were responsible for the training of a Japanese pilot during the summer of 1972.

Schütte-Lanz Ships

The German company Luftschiffbau Schütte-Lanz of Mannheim-Rheinau produced a number of rigid airships of an advanced design. These ships were streamlined and were constructed of laminated plywood girders instead of the aluminium used on the Zeppelin craft. The wooden girders were formed in a diamond-shaped pattern, making the ships very robust. A significant feature of these airships were the monoplane tail fins. About twenty Schütte-Lanz ships were projected or built. Many aspects of the design developed by the Schütte-Lanz company were used on the later Zeppelin airships.

Schütte-Lanz 1, the first wooden rigid airship

Schütte-Lanz 2

GERMAN NON-RIGID AND SEMI-RIGID AIRSHIPS

Class/Name	Make/Type	Launched	Vol. (cu.ft.)	Dimensions (ft) Length	Diam.	Engines No.(hp each)	Speed max. mph	Remarks
Baumergarten and Wolfert	(NR)	1879	—	59.6	19.6	3 hand-driven	—	Tested without result at Charlottenburg 5.3.82.
Clouth	Clouth (SR)	1909	65,342	138.6	28.05	1 Adler (50)	22.37	Had wooden supports for car suspension, laced on sides of envelope, and so was really a semi-rigid airship.
Erbsloen/Leichlingen	Erbsloen (NR)	1909	102,428	185.5	33	1 Benz (28)	25	Exploded on 13.7.10 killing her crew of five.
Güldenring/ Ex-Underberg	Goodyear/Ballon Fabrik (NR)	1959	158,895	160.05	42.2	2 Warrel (145)	—	Given larger envelope 1958. Became *Schwab* in 1961.
Hildebrandt/Baldwin II	Baldwin (NR)	1909	20,000	96	19.6	1 Curtis (20)	19.61	Copy of the U.S. *Baldwin I.*
Kiel 1	Steffens (SR)	1910	17,700	103	—	1 Buchet (40)	—	Flew three miles on first ascent.
Ma (or Gross)	German Military Airship Works (SR)	1907	63,558	131.2	26.9	1 Geggenham (24)	20	Designed by Herr Basenach at Tegel Airship Factory. Similar to Lebaudy semi-rigid airships. Trimming by chain. Propellers were in line with the keel. Experimental craft.
M I	Airship Works (SR)	1907	176,550	214.9	36.4	2 (75)	28.6	The keel of this airship was in three linked parts. The envelope was enlarged to 194,200 cu.ft.
M II	Airship Works (SR)	1909	194,200	—	—	—	—	*MII* was *MI* enlarged and modified.
M III	Airship Works (SR)	1909	275,418	267.4	42.7	4 Körting (75)	36.7	Trimming by air in ballonets and movement of water in tanks. Later enlarged.
M IV	Airship Works (SR)	1911	388,410	315	45.9	2 (200)	38	Had two cars at first but was not successful and so was reconstructed and enlarged.

Class/Name	Make/Type	Launched	Vol. (cu.ft.)	Dimensions (ft) Length	Diam.	Engines No.(hp each)	Speed max. mph	Remarks
Ersatz M IV (enlarged)	Airship Works (SR)	1913	476,685	323.1	50.19	3 (160)	51.2	The keel was attached directly under envelope, therefore she had no external suspension. Enlarged to 688,740 cu.ft. in 1914. Was employed by navy on coastal patrol.
PV	Parseval (NR)	1906	81,130	164	29.5	1 Daimler (85)	26.8	Enlarged to 96,868 cu.ft. Became *PL1*.
PL1	Parseval (NR)	1909	112,992	196.8	31	1 Daimler (85)	26.8	Was *PV*, the experimental ship. Enlarged and modified.
PL2/Type A	Parseval (NR)	1908	141,240	196.8	34.1	1 Daimler (85)	27.9	Built for the army. Became *P1*.
PL3/Type B	Parseval (NR)	1909	233,046	229.6	40.3	2 NAG (100)	31.8	Military *PII*.
PL4/Type B	Parseval (NR)	1909	81,206	165	28.21	Austro-Daimler (75)	27.92	Built in Austria for the Austrian Army.
PL5	Parseval (NR)	1909	51,199	131.2	26.2	1 Daimler (25)	20.16	Spat airship. Enlarged to 282,480 cu.ft. Made 250 passenger flights and carried 2,300 passengers over 9,326 miles. Useful lift 6,600lb.
PL6	Parseval (NR)	1910	240,108	229	40.3	2 NAG (110)	33.5	She had non-rigid fabric propellers. Became passenger-carrying *Stollwerck*.
PL7/Grifr	Parseval (NR)	1910	268,390	236.1	46	2 NAG (110)	36.7	Bought by Russian Army.
PL8/Ersatz P2	Parseval (NR)	1912	291,225	252.5	50.85	2 Maybach (170-80)	40.9	Construction began in 1910 but not completed until 1912.
PL9 and PL10	Parseval (NR)	1910(?)	60,072	131.2	26.2	1 Körting (50)	24.6	Enlarged and bought by the Turkish Army.
PL11	Parseval (NR)	1911	353,100	275.5	51	2 Körting (200)	40.3	Became *PIII*.

GERMAN NON-RIGID AND SEMI-RIGID AIRSHIPS

Class/Name	Make/Type	Launched	Vol. (cu.ft.)	Dimensions (ft) Length	Diam.	Engines No.(hp each)	Speed max. mph	Remarks
PL12/Charlotte	Parseval (NR)	1912	282,480	269	45.9	2 NAG (110)	33.5	Became passenger ship of the Rhenish Westphalian Air Sport Company.
PL13	Parseval (NR)	1912	282,480	259.2	47.6	2 Maybach (150)	41.2	Japanese army airship.
PL14	Parseval (NR)	1913	353,100	278.8	53.5	2 Maybach (180)	41.4	Russian army airship.
PL15	Parseval (NR)	1912	353,100	278.8	53.5	2 Maybach (180)	—	Italian army airship. Dimensions uncertain, but are almost the same as those for *PL14*, *PL16*, and the German army's *P4*.
PL16/PLIV	Parseval (NR)	1914	353,100	308.3	50.8	2 Maybach (180)	47.1	German army designation *PLIV*.
PL17	Parseval (NR)	1912	353,100	278.8	52.5	2 Maybach (170)	40.3	Italian army airship. First Parseval with "trajectory based suspension".
PL18/NA4	Parseval (NR)	1913	300,135	275.5	49.2	2 Maybach (180)	40.3	Became British Naval Airship *No. 4*. Afterwards enlarged and was given wooden propellers instead of metal S-R propellers. This resulted in a gain in speed to about 45 mph.
PL19	Parseval (NR)	1914	363,693	308.3	51.2	2 Maybach (180)	47.9	On order for England but taken over by German Army, then handed over to German Navy. Destroyed at sea after bombing raid in 1915.
PL20 and 21/ Parseval 6 and 7	Parseval (NR)	*P6* 1915, *P7* 1917	353,100	301.8	47.2	2 Maybach (180)	42.5 (*P6* later 60)	P7 made one flight then was used for spares P5 and P6. P6 was reconstructed with a resultant increase in speed.

Class/Name	Make/Type	Launched	Vol. (cu.ft.)	Dimensions (ft) Length	Diam.	Engines No.(hp each)	Speed max. mph	Remarks
								Both originally had swivel propellers.
PL25	Parseval (NR)	1915	473,154	368.7	58.7	2 Maybach (210)	43.68	Naval patrol craft.
PL26	Parseval (SR)	1915	1,059,300	511.7	62.6	4 Maybach (210)	50.3	First Parseval semi-rigid airship. Burnt in shed 19.11.15. Did not complete trials.
PL27	Parseval (SR)	1917	1,105,203	518.2	64.3	4 Maybach (240)	56	Built for German navy but not used on operations.
PN28/Trumpf I	Parseval-Natz (SR)	1928	60,027	130	25.5	1 Siemens Halske (80)	50	Employed by Trumpf Chocolate. Made 1,200 flights.
(Alternative figures for Trumpf I)	Parseval-Natz (SR)	1926	43,000	72	—	1 Siemens (120)	—	End of useful life 1933.
PN29	Parseval-Natz (SR)	1930	77,682	—	—	1 Siemens Halske (100)	56	Could carry five passengers. Moored to a mast at Stockholm in 1930. Made 200 flights (600 hrs). Came down in the Baltic while flying home. Crew saved.
PN30	Parseval-Natz (SR)	1932	91,806	151	35.6 (Height 52.6)	1 Siemens Halske (115)	49.75	Made 550 fiights up to 1934. Spent 63 days non-stop on the mast. Spent total of 135 days on the mast. Used for passenger carrying and advertising.
Schwab/Ex-Güldenring	Enlarged Goodyear "L" class (NR)	1961	158,895	160.05	42.2	2 Warner (145)	—	*Güldenring* was sold to Japan on 24.4.68. Known as the *Flying Dragon*. Wrecked due to mast failure on 4.4.69.

GERMAN NON-RIGID AND SEMI-RIGID AIRSHIPS

Class/Name	Make/Type	Launched	Vol. (cu.ft.)	Dimensions (ft) Length	Diam.	Engines No.(hp each)	Speed max. mph	Remarks
Trumpf II	Ballonfabrik Augsburg (NR)	1956	189,728	188.1	43.5	1 Franklin (215)	48.4	Made 26 flights, flying 43 hours and was deflated when mooring mast collapsed in a gale at Stuttgart in 1957. Not flown again.
Trumpf III	Ballonfabrik and Metallwerk (NR)	1958	158,895	159.3	43.3	2 Warner Scarab (180)	68	The first German airship to be inflated with helium. Launched at Stuttgart and rigged in the open air. Flown as the *Braun Sixtant* in 1969. Taken over by WDL in 1970 and was based at Mulheim-Ruhr. She was fitted with an auxiliary blower and had reversible propellers. Useful lift 4,224lb.
Underberg (L.19)	Goodyear "L" class (NR)	1956	123,000	150	46	2 Warner (145)	63	Launched as U.S. Navy *L19* in 1947. Enlarged in 1959 and became *Güldenring*.
Ruthenberg I	Ruthenberg (SR)	1909	42,372	131.2	21.3	1 Benz (24)	22.4	Tubular steel keel was closely attached to the envelope. Belonged to Herr Haase of Hamburg. Flown at the Frankfurt airship exhibition of 1909.
Ruthenberg II	Ruthenberg (SR)	1911	60,027	150.8	24.2	1 Fiat (75)	22.4	A moveable weight was used in lieu of elevator planes for trimming. She was damaged while landing in 1911.

Class/Name	Make/Type	Launched	Vol. (cu.ft.)	Dimensions (ft) Length	Diam.	Engines No.(hp each)	Speed max. mph	Remarks
Schukert	Siemens (NR)	1911	476,685	393.6	44.3	4 Daimler (120)	44.3	Made 73 flights in one and a half years. The longest of these was a five-hour flight over a distance of 500km. She was rebuilt and bought by the army and deleted soon after.
Suchard I	Rerdingen, MB, Lürssen (NR)	1911	343,466	199.6	(width 56.7)	2 NAG (110) + 1 SU Auxiliary (6)	27.5	Built for Brucker Trans Atlantic Flight Exhibition. Enlarged after trials.
Suchard IA	Rerdingen and Lurssen (NR)	1913	423,600	250.8	(width 56.7)	2 NAG (110) + 1 SU Auxiliary (6)	25	Lengthened *Suchard I*. After trials the intended trans Atlantic flight was abandoned and the ship was dismantled. The car consisted of a motor boat hull.
V1	Deutche Luftschift Werft (SR)	1911	236,792.5	231	(width 40.9)	2 Schreeweis (180)	37.5	*V1* or *V2* had a long external keel running from bow to stern, which was not covered in. *V1* enlarged to 250.8ft. in length. Flew again in 1913.
V2	Deutche Luftschift Werft (SR)	1913	423,600	250.8	(width 40.9)	2 Mercedes (130)	42.5	Made a number of flights, then broken up because of lack of funds.
Woelfert	Woelfert (NR)	1886	28,248	91.8	27.8	1 Benzine (8)	—	The engine was cooled by iced water. She was very unsatisfactory on trials, 28-29.8.86, and again in 1887. Woelfert made a benzine vapouriser which was situated close to the

Trumpf II. She was not flown after her mooring mast collapsed in a gale in 1957

Trumpf III passing the mast at Kassel in 1959. She was bought by WDL and flown as the *Braun Sixtant.* This was the first airship in Europe to be inflated with helium.

The car and engines of *Trumpf III*

Class/Name	Make/Type	Launched	Vol. (cu.ft.)	Dimensions (ft) Length	Diam.	Engines No.(hp each)	Speed max. mph	Remarks
								envelope and set it on fire. The airship exploded, according the doubtful honour to Woelfert and Knabe, of being the first men to be killed in an airship accident (14.6.87).
WDL1 (serial No.100)/ The Flying Muskateer (renamed Wicküler)	Westdeutsche Luftwerbung (NR)	1972	211,888	180.5	47.85	2 Rolls Royce (180)	62	After orders for WDL1 ships have been met, production of WDL2 ships will proceed.
WDL1 (serial No. 101)	Westdeutsche Luftwerbung (NR)	1972	211,888	180.5	47.85	2 Rolls Royce (180)	62	Sold to the Orient Lease Co of Japan. Useful lift 3,300lb.

Schwab, the enlarged Goodyear "L" class ship, was formerly the *Güldenring*, which previously was known as the *Underberg*

Flying Musketeer at Mulheim

Zeppelins

It was Count Ferdinand von Zeppelin who conceived and developed the first rigid airships. His imagination was fired by a paper written by the German Postmaster-General on "World Mail and Airship Travel", and when in 1884 he heard of the success of the small French airship *La France*, he decided that Germany should not be left behind.

The Count set about designing his airship, and his first proposal, for an "aerial express train", was examined by a technical commission headed by Professor Hermann von Helmholz in 1894. The commission found the Count's design to be utterly impractical and advised wisely against spending government money on it.

With Count Ferdinand von Zeppelin at the controls, *LZ1* made its maiden flight on 2 July 1900

LZ 2 moored on Lake Constance

The Count's next step was to seek the assistance of Professor Müller-Breslau, a member of the commission, and the result of their co-operation was the development of what became the typical Zeppelin cigar-shaped airship. This new configuration consisted of a light and strong structure composed of internally braced transverse rings. Professor Müller-Breslau never received any credit for the assistance he rendered to the Count.

In May 1894 the "Joint Stock Company for Promotion of Airship Flight" was formed, and shortly afterwards work began on *Luftschiff Zeppelin 1* (*LZ 1*). This airship was built in a floating shed on Lake Constance. The first flight of *LZ 1* took place on 2 July 1900 and only two more flights were made as the ship lacked sufficient speed and control. *LZ 1* was broken up in 1901, and it was not until 1905 that the Count began construction of *LZ 2*. This, his second airship, was destroyed on her second flight.

Undeterred by the loss of *LZ 2* the Count used the last of his private fortune to build *LZ 3*, which was completed in 1906. This ship was in part a success, making a record flight of 8 hours, which impressed the German Army sufficiently for them to agree to the purchase of a ship, but only if certain tests could be passed; namely, that the ship must be able to stay in the air for 24 hours, cover a distance of 435 miles and return to her base having reached a specified destination. As *LZ 3* did not have the required capabilities to make this flight, the Count started work on *LZ 4*, which he completed in June 1908.

LZ 3, the first military Zeppelin

LZ 4, destroyed by fire on 5 August 1908

LZ 6 made her first flight on 25 August 1909, and was later taken over by DELAG and enlarged. She was burnt in her shed on 14 August 1910

LZ 4 was wrecked in a storm during the trials held for the army, which instead of making an end of the Count's career, prompted him to renewed action. Voluntary contributions came from all over Germany and, with these donations, amounting to over £300,000, the Count set up the "Zeppelin Foundation for the Promotion of Aerial Navigation".

At last a measure of success came with *LZ 5*, and the War Ministry purchased *LZ 3* and *LZ 5*; a further ship, *LZ 6*, built in anticipation of more orders, remained unsold. However, it was the completion of the *Schwaben* in 1911 that brought about a dramatic change in the Count's fortune. In 11 months the *Schwaben*, *LZ 10*, carried 1,533 passengers on a total of 218 flights, and she became known as "the lucky ship of the DELAG". This was an acronym for Deutsche Luftschiffahrts-Aktien-Gesellschaft, the airship transport company set up in Frankfurt in 1909.

The *Schwaben* was destroyed by fire in a violent gale, but fortunately all her passengers and crew managed to disembark safely. Meanwhile, the DELAG fleet was growing with the additions of the *Viktoria Luise*, *Sachsen* and *Hansa* being made in 1912 and 1913.

The ships of the DELAG fleet were not only engaged in passenger carrying, for the German Navy's first airship crews were trained aboard the *Viktoria Luise* and *Hansa*, often flying them while passengers were aboard. The first Navy airship was ordered on 24 April 1912 and, when built, was kept at a rented DELAG hangar until the Nordholz base was fully developed.

Count Zeppelin was not alone in his pioneering activities, for the Luftschiffbau Schütte-Lanz of Mannheim-Rheinau was set up in competition with his company. The firm was founded in 1909 by Dr Johann Schütte, a professor at the University of Danzig (now Gdańsk), and a group of industrialists, and found favour with the German War Ministry, which encouraged competition with the Zeppelin Company. The firm of Schütte-Lanz proposed to build rigid airships of laminated plywood girders, and their first ship, the *SL 1*, launched on 17 October 1911, was bought by the German Army. *SL 2* was completed in 1914, and had a streamlined hull with cruciform

LZ 7, the *Deutschland*, wrecked at Teutoburger Wald on 28 June 1910

LZ 10, the *Schwaben* flying near her shed at Dusseldorf

fins, rudders and elevators fitted at the stern. The control car was fully enclosed, and the engines were directy coupled to the propellers. The ship embodied many other novel features which were later used in the Zeppelins. These advances were patented by the Schütte-Lanz Company, but were later taken over by the German Government.

In March 1914 an order was placed for a new naval airship, the Zeppelin design being chosen in preference to Professor Schütte's submission. The Schütte-Lanz airship would have suited the Navy's requirements better than the *L 3*, but Professor Schütte was not liked by Grand Admiral Alfred von Tirpitz, the Secretary of State for the Navy. It was Admiral von Tirpitz who established the German Navy as a force of primary importance in world affairs. Many of the Schütte-Lanz advances in design were later incorporated into the airships of the Zeppelin Company, but it is not true that all these features were copied directly from the Schütte-Lanz model.

By 1913 the German Navy was committed to a programme of expansion which laid the foundations for the airship service. The German Navy's airships made over 700 raids over the North Sea and the Baltic between 1914 and 1918, with a loss of 106 ships, which in retrospect seems out of all proportion to the damage caused by the bombing of Britain, amounting to just over 3 million pounds sterling. The Zeppelin raiders can be regarded as the first strategic bombing force in the world.

The DELAG ship *Viktoria Luise*

Ersatz L 1, landing in winter snows

At the end of the war DELAG was taken over by Baron Gemmingen, who was Count Zeppelin's nephew and took over the company following his uncle's death in 1917. Together with Dr Hugo Eckener he made plans to expand the company's commercial activities, and soon the *L 72*, originally destined for the Navy, was joined by *LZ 120*, the *Bodensee*. The success of the post-war operations of DELAG prompted the construction of a new airship, the *Nordstern*, which was ready for service in January 1920, but the Allies, who had already taken the surviving Navy airships at the end of the war, demanded the DELAG fleet as further reparation. So *L 72* went to France and became the *Dixmude*, as did the *Nordstern* which was

LZ 18, the Naval Airship *L2*, which was the only ship of the "I" class

L 9. This was the first ship to be built with ten-metre spacing of her transverse frames

renamed *Méditerranée*, and the *Bodensee* was sent to Italy. *L 64* and *L 71* were flown to the Norfolk base of Pulham in England.

In order to avoid financial ruin, DELAG officials approached the Americans and offered to build an airship for the U.S. Navy. After approval for construction was obtained from America's allies, the company set to work. *LZ 126*, known in the United States as *ZR-3* or *Los Angeles*, was completed in September 1924 and, after a number of tests, took off from Friedrichshafen for America on 13 October 1924. The ship arrived at Lakehurst, N.J., on the 16th.

Plans were then laid for the construction of the *Graf Zeppelin*, which was funded by public subscription and a grant from the German Government. The successful career of this giant airship started with a flight to America, which took 111 hours and 43 minutes. The return journey was made in a record 71 hours and 7 minutes.

The rest of the *Graf Zeppelin's* career was as eventful and as colourful as it was long. One of her most interesting voyages was a trans-Siberian flight, which took her over the Ural Mountains, over Soviet Asia and the vast swamps around the Yenisei River, to the then uncharted Stanovoi Mountains, which was the most dangerous part of her journey. On the journey over this mountain range Hugo Eckener piloted his ship with consummate skill through a narrow canyon, taking her almost to her pressure height. Eventually the *Graf Zeppelin* crossed the crest of the mountains and made her way over the Sea of Okhotsk to Japan. This was the first non-stop flight over Russia.

Stern view of *LZ 22*

LZ 62, the naval *L30*

From Tokyo in Japan the *Graf Zeppelin* went on to America, calling at Los Angeles, finally completing her round-the-world flight on 29 August 1929 when she arrived back at Lakehurst, her starting point. The whole journey had taken 21 days, 7 hours and 34 minutes, of which 7 days, 5 hours and 54 minutes had been spent at her ports of call. She had started her journey from Lakehurst on 8 August at 5.42 a.m.

L3 of the "M" class

A Zeppelin tail gunner's position. The giant rudder can be seen behind the gunner

The "R" class airship *L 41*, painted black for night raiding

In 1929 the *Graf Zeppelin* carried out a survey in the Arctic, and in July 1930 she pioneered a regular service to South America. The future now looked full of promise for Eckener and DELAG, but the *Hindenburg* disaster put an end to the career of the *Graf Zeppelin*. She was broken up in 1940 after spending nine years in service, in which time the only serious mechanical defect suffered was when two of her engines broke down over France in 1929.

LZ 77, the first Zeppelin to be shot down in flames

One of *L 33's* propellers, showing the outrigger construction for the drive. *L 33* was shot down near Little Wigborough in Essex on the night of 23/24 September 1916

L 48, the first Zeppelin to have a streamlined control car

One of the first streamlined rear-engine gondolas was fitted on *L 44*. The gondola in the illustration contained two engines which were geared to a pusher propeller

The control car of *L 54*

A bow view of the "W" class ship *L 59* leaving her shed

L 53, Type "V" (*LZ 100*). The white area on the top of the ship was designed to reduce superheating of the lifting gas

L 70 being walked into a shed at Friedrichshafen

The port side of the control car on *L 59*, showing the elevator control wheel, inclinometer, altimeter, and the water-ballast and gas valve controls

The bomb-sight, electrical bomb release switches and the rudder chains in the control car of *L59*

L65 wrecked by her crew at Nordholz on 23 June 1919

LZ 120, the *Bodensee*

LZ 129, the *Hindenburg*, which caught fire as it approached the mooring mast at Lakehurst, N.J., on 6 May 1937

Construction of *LZ 129* started at the end of 1934, and the *Hindenburg* as this ship was called, was designed to be the safest airship yet built: her motors were to be fed with crude oil, not petrol; the catwalks were being covered with layers of rubber and her crew members who worked near the gas cells were to wear asbestos suits; the smoking-room was fire-proofed and matches and lighters were to be confiscated from all who came aboard. She was to be filled with helium but the Americans refused to let the militaristic Nazi Government have any, and consequently her gas bags had to be inflated with hydrogen.

Despite all the stringent safety measures, the *Hindenburg* was destroyed in the dreadful accident at Lakehurst in May 1937. Out of the 97 crew and passengers on board, 62 escaped. Of those who died, 22 were crew members.

A Board of Inquiry was set up which included Dr Eckener, and the final analysis was made by him and accepted by the Americans and

LZ 127, the *Graf Zeppelin 1*

Germans. His view was that one of the stern cells developed a leak, and that the escaping hydrogen had been ignited by static electricity. This then produced an explosion which resulted in a chain reaction, setting fire to the whole ship. However, there is a school of thought that believes the real cause of the tragedy may well have been sabotage. Max Pruss, the captain of the *Hindenburg*, firmly believed this to be the case as did a number of the U.S. Navy's most experienced airship pilots.

LZ 130, the last of the German rigid airships, was at this time nearing completion at Friedrichshafen, and by September 1938 was completed. This ship was named the *Graf Zeppelin II* and made her first flight, inflated with hydrogen, on 14 September, but after a few more flights was grounded on the orders of Hitler and was broken up during 1940.

Graf Zeppelin II, which was scrapped in March 1940 on orders from Marshal Göring, the metal from the framework being used to build heavier-than-air machines

Schwarz's *Metallballon* which made its first flight on 3 November 1897

This rare photograph shows a most distinguished gathering of Austro-German aristocracy and aeronautical expertise in the car of a Parseval airship. From left to right: Oskar von Miller, the famous engineer; Prince Ludwig of Bavaria, later King Ludwig III; Graf Ferdinand von Zeppelin; and Major von Parseval. The group is flanked by two military personnel

A dining room on board the *Graf Zeppelin I*

The Hindenburg exploding into flames at Lakenhurst while she was attempting to land on 6 May 1937. Water ballast tanks can be seen falling from the ship

GERMAN RIGID AIRSHIPS

Class/Name	Make/Type	Launched	Vol. (cu.ft.)	Dimensions (ft) Length	Diam.	Engines No.(hp each)	Speed max. mph	Remarks
Schwartz	Rigid with metal cover	1897	130,541	156	47.5	1 Daimler (12)	—	On her first flight on 3.11.1897 the propeller belt slipped and the ship made no headway in a 16mph wind. A balloon landing was then made with little damage to the ship, but a rising wind and the spectators destroyed the ship. The *Schwartz Metalballon* was piloted by a soldier.
SL1	Schütte-Lanz	1911	688,545	430	60.3	2 Mercedes (240)	42.4	First wooden rigid airship.
SL2	Schütte-Lanz	1914	881,690	472	59.7	4 Maybach (180)	54.6	German Army ship employed on the East and West Fronts. Wrecked in a storm on 10.1.16.
SL3	Schütte-Lanz	1915	1,144,044	502.4	65	4 Maybach (210)	57.7	Naval airship. Crashed 1.5.16.
SL4	Schütte-Lanz	1915	1,146,500	502.4	65	4 Maybach (210)	52.8	Naval airship. Different gondola arrangement from *SL3*. Blown out of shed and wrecked in 1915.
SL5	Schütte-Lanz	1915	1,146,500	502.4	65	4 Maybach (210)	57	Army ship wrecked after forced landing in a gale on 5.7.15.
SL6	Schütte-Lanz	1915	1,235,850	534.5	64.10	4 Maybach (210)	57.9	Naval ship. Exploded on 18.11.15. No survivors.
SL7	Schütte-Lanz	1915	1,235,850	534.5	64.10	4 Maybach (210)	57.9	Deleted when army gave up airships 6.3.17.
SL8	Schütte-Lanz	1916	1,366,497	570.10	65.11	4 Maybach (240)	57.7	Naval ship. Dismantled November 1917.
SL9	Schütte-Lanz	1916	1,366,497	570.10	65.11	4 Maybach (240)	57.7	Naval ship. Burned in air in

Class/Name	Make/Type	Launched	Vol. (cu.ft.)	Dimensions (ft) Length	Diam.	Engines No.(hp each)	Speed max. mph	Remarks
								thunderstorm near Pillau.
SL10	Schütte-Lanz	1916	1,366,497	570.10	65.11	4 Maybach (240)	57.7	Army ship. Disappeared over Black Sea 28.7.16.
SL11	Schütte-Lanz	1916	1,366,497	570.10	65.11	4 Maybach (240)	57.7	Army ship. Shot down over London on 2.8.16. No survivors.
SL12	Schütte-Lanz	1916	1,366,497	570.10	65.11	4 Maybach (240)	57.7	Naval ship. Wrecked in forced landing.
SL13	Schütte-Lanz	1916	1,366,497	570.10	65.11	4 Maybach (240)	57.7	Army ship. Burnt in works at Leipzig 28.12.16.
SL14	Schütte-Lanz	1916	1,366,497	570.10	65.11	4 Maybach (240)	57.7	Naval ship. Dismantled May 1917.
SL15	Schütte-Lanz	1916	1,366,497	570.10	65.11	4 Maybach (240)	57.7	Army ship. Deleted in 1917
SL16	Schütte-Lanz	1917	1,366,497	570.10	65.11	4 Maybach (240)	57.7	Army ship. Deleted in 1917.
SL17	Schütte-Lanz	1917	1,366,497	570.10	65.11	4 Maybach (240)	57.7	Army ship. Deleted in 1917
SL18 and 19	Schütte-Lanz	1917	1,366,497	570.10	65.11	4 Maybach (240)	—	Not completed. SL framework burnt at Leipzig.
SL20	Schütte-Lanz	1917	1,989,700	651	75.3	5 Maybach (240)	62.8	Naval ship. Destroyed in explosion in shed.
SL21 and 22	Schütte-Lanz	1918	1,977,360	650	75.1	5 Maybach (240)	62.6	Not completed.
LZ1	Zeppelin/A	1900	399,003	420	38.2	2 Daimler (14.7)	17.3	Ship broken up early in 1901 after three flights.
LZ2	Zeppelin/B	1905	399,003	420	38.2	2 Daimler (85)	24.6	Destroyed in gale 18.1.06.
LZ3 (became Z1)	Zeppelin/B	1906	430,782	446	38.4	2 Daimler (115)	27.2	First Military "Zeppelin". Purchased in 1909. Deleted spring 1913.
LZ4	Zeppelin/C	1908	529,650	446	42.6	2 Daimler (105)	29.7	Destroyed by fire on 5.8.08.
LZ5 (became Z II)	Zeppelin/C	1909	529,650	446	42.6	2 Daimler (105)	29.7	Destroyed after forced landing on 10.5.10.
LZ6	Zeppelin/D	1909	564,960	472	42.6	1 Maybach (145) 2 Daimler (115)	37.5	With *LZ6*, Count Zeppelin founded the world's first commercial airline, DELAG.

GERMAN RIGID AIRSHIPS

Class/Name	Make/Type	Launched	Vol. (cu.ft.)	Dimensions (ft) Length	Diam.	Engines No.(hp each)	Speed max. mph	Remarks
LZ7/Deutchland	Zeppelin/E	1910	681,483	485.4	45.9	3 Daimler (120)	37.2	Burnt in shed 14.9.10. Wrecked in a gale at Teutoburger Wald while carrying 20 passengers on 28.6.10. No injuries.
LZ8/Ersatz Deutchland	Zeppelin/E	1911	681,483	485.4	45.9	3 Daimler (120)	37.2	Wrecked while docking on 16.5.11. No casualties.
LZ9	Zeppelin/F	1911	628,518	459.2	45.9	3 Maybach (145)	38.4	Replacement for *ZII*. Deleted on 1.8.14 after 150 flights.
LZ10/Schwäben	Zeppelin/F	1911	628,518	459.2	45.9	3 Maybach (145)	47.1	DELAG ship. Burnt in shed on 28.6.12.
LZ11/Viktoria Luise	Zeppelin/G	1912	670,900	485.4	45.9	3 Maybach (150)	48.9	DELAG ship. Wrecked while docking on 1.10.15.
LZ12 (Z III)	Zeppelin/F	1912	628,518	459.2	45.9	3 Maybach (145)	47.1	Military ship and sister to *LZ10*. Deleted summer 1914.
LZ13/Hansa	Zeppelin/G	1912	670,900	484.5	45.9	3 Maybach (150)	48.9	DELAG ship. Deleted summer 1915.
LZ14 (L1)	Zeppelin/H	1912	793,239	518.2	48.7	3 Maybach (165)	49.6	First naval ship. Crashed in N. Sea. 9.9.13.
LZ15 (EZ1)	Zeppelin/H	1913	793,239	518.2	48.7	3 Maybach (165)	49.6	—
LZ16 (Z IV)	Zeppelin/H	1913	793,239	518.2	48.7	3 Maybach (165)	49.6	Deleted spring 1916.
LZ17/Sachsen	Zeppelin/H	1913	793,239	518.2	48.7	3 Maybach (165)	49.6	DELAG ship taken over by army. Became naval school ship and enlarged. Deleted 6.9.16.
LZ18 (L2)	Zeppelin/I	1913	953,370	518.2	54.5	4 Maybach (180)	48.9	Internal keel and separate control car. Burned in air on 17.10.13.
LZ19 (EZ1)	Zeppelin/H	1913	793,239	518.2	48.7	3 Maybach (180)	49.6	Stranded 13.6.14. No injuries.
LZ20 (Z V)	Zeppelin/H	—	793,239	518.2	48.7	3 Maybach (180)	49.6	Later enlarged.

Class/Name	Make/Type	Launched	Vol. (cu.ft.)	Dimensions (ft) Length	Diam.	Engines No.(hp each)	Speed max. mph	Remarks
LZ21 (Z VI)	Zeppelin/K	1913	729,024	485.4	48.7	3 Maybach (180)	46.5	Hit by gunfire and made a forced landing near Bonn on 18.6.14. No injuries.
LZ22 (Z VII)	Zeppelin/L	1914	781,763	511.7	48.7	3 Maybach (180)	44.6	Shot down on 23.8.14.
LZ23 (Z VIII)	Zeppelin/L	1914	781,763	511.7	48.7	3 Maybach (180)	44.6	Shot down on 23.8.14.
LZ24 (L3)	Zeppelin/M	1914	793,415	518.2	48.7	3 Maybach (210)	52	Stranded on Danish coast on 17.2.15.
LZ25 (Z IX)	Zeppelin/M	1914	793,415	518.2	48.7	3 Maybach (210)	47.4	Bombed in shed at Dusseldorf on 8.10.14.
LZ26 (Z XII)	Zeppelin/N	1914	882,750	528.7	52.4	3 Maybach (210)	50.2	Deleted on 8.8.17.
LZ27 (L4)	Zeppelin/M	1914	793,415	518.2	48.7	3 Maybach (210)	51.4	First cruciform fins and rudders. Lost in forced landing 17.2.16.
LZ28 (L5)	Zeppelin/M	1914	793,415	518.2	48.7	3 Maybach (210)	52.1	Damaged by gunfire over Russia. Dismantled 16.8.15.
LZ29 (Z X)	Zeppelin/M	1914	793,415	518.2	48.7	3 Maybach (210)	52	—
LZ30 (Z XI)	Zeppelin/M	1914	793,415	518.2	48.7	3 Maybach (210)	52	—
LZ31 (L6)	Zeppelin/M	1914	793,415	518.2	48.7	3 Maybach (210)	52	Burned in shed 16.9.16.
LZ32 (L7)	Zeppelin/M	1914	793,415	518.2	48.7	3 Maybach (210)	52	Shot down by cruisers *Galetea* and *Phaeton*. Finished off by submarine *E.31*, 4.5.16.
LZ33 (L8)	Zeppelin/M	1914	793,415	518.2	48.7	3 Maybach (210)	52	Lost in forced landing after gunfire damage.
LZ34	Zeppelin/M	1915	793,415	518.2	48.7	3 Maybach (210)	52	—
LZ35	Zeppelin/M	1915	793,415	518.2	48.7	3 Maybach (210)	52	—
LZ36 (L9)	Zeppelin/O	1915	879,219	529.3	52.4	3 Maybach (210)	51.4	Burnt in shed with *L6* on 16.9.16.
LZ37	Zeppelin/M	1915	793,415	518.2	48.7	3 Maybach (210)	52	—
LZ38	Zeppelin/P	1915	1,126,389	536.2	61.3	4 Maybach (210)	60.1	—
LZ39	Zeppelin/O	1915	879,219	529.3	52.4	3 Maybach (210)	51.4	Forced landing after raid and wrecked 13-14.10.15.

GERMAN RIGID AIRSHIPS

Class/Name	Make/Type	Launched	Vol. (cu.ft.)	Dimensions (ft) Length	Diam.	Engines No.(hp each)	Speed max. mph	Remarks
LZ40 (L10)	Zeppelin/P	1915	1,126,389	536.2	61.3	4 Maybach (210)	60.1	Struck by lightning and destroyed on 3.9.15.
LZ41 (L11)	Zeppelin/P	1915	1,126,389	536.2	61.3	4 Maybach (210)	60.1	Deleted on 25.4.17. Dismantled on 24.11.17.
LZ42 (LZ72)	Zeppelin/P	1915	1,126,389	536.2	61.3	4 Maybach (210)	60.1	—
LZ43 (L12)	Zeppelin/P	1915	1,126,389	536.2	61.3	4 Maybach (210)	60.1	Damaged by gunfire off England and was burned while being dismantled on 10.8.15.
LZ44 (LZ74)	Zeppelin/P	1915	1,126,389	536.2	61.3	4 Maybach (210)	60.1	—
LZ45 (L13)	Zeppelin/P	1915	1,126,389	536.2	61.3	4 Maybach (210)	60.1	Dismantled on 11.12.17.
LZ46 (L14)	Zeppelin/P	1915	1,126,389	536.2	61.3	4 Maybach (210)	60.1	Wrecked by airship crews on 23.6.19.
LZ47 (LZ77)	Zeppelin/P	1915	1,126,389	536.2	61.3	4 Maybach (210)	60.1	Shot down on raid on 21.2.16. First Zeppelin to be set on fire.
LZ48 (L15)	Zeppelin/P	1915	1,126,389	536.2	61.3	4 Maybach (210)	60.1	Shot down in sea and sank on 1.4.16.
LZ49 (LZ79)	Zeppelin/P	1915	1,126,389	536.2	61.3	4 Maybach (210)	60.1	—
LZ50 (L16)	Zeppelin/P	1915	1,126,389	536.2	61.3	4 Maybach (210)	60.1	Wrecked on landing on 19.10.17.
LZ51* (LZ81)	Zeppelin/P	1915	1,126,389	536.2	61.3	4 Maybach (210)	60.1	Enlarged.
LZ52 (L18)	Zeppelin/P	1915	1,126,389	536.2	61.3	4 Maybach (210)	60.1	Burned in shed on 17.11.15.
LZ53 (L17)	Zeppelin/P	1915	1,126,389	536.2	61.3	4 Maybach (210)	60.1	Burned in shed with *LZ4* on 28.12.16.
LZ54 (L19)	Zeppelin/P	1915	1,126,389	536.2	61.3	4 Maybach (210)	60.1	Lost in N. Sea after a raid on England on 2.2.16.
LZ55 (LZ85)	Zeppelin/P	1915	1,126,389	536.2	61.3	4 Maybach (210)	60.1	Enlarged.
LZ56* (LZ86)	Zeppelin/P	1915	1,126,389	536.2	61.3	4 Maybach (210)	60.1	Enlarged.
LZ57* (LZ87)	Zeppelin/P	1915	1,126,389	536.2	61.3	4 Maybach (210)	60.1	Enlarged.
LZ58* (LZ88)	Zeppelin/P	1915	1,126,389	536.2	61.3	4 Maybach (210)	60.1	Enlarged.

Class/Name	Make/Type	Launched	Vol. (cu.ft.)	Dimensions (ft) Length	Diam.	Engines No.(hp each)	Speed max. mph	Remarks
LZ59 (L20)	Zeppelin/Q	1916	1,126,389	585	61.3	4 Maybach (240)	58.9	Enlarged. Made a forced landing in Norway after a raid on England.
LZ60* (LZ90)	Zeppelin/P	1915	1,359,433	.536.2	61.3	4 Maybach (210)	60.1	Enlarged to the same dimensions as *LZ51*, *56* and *57* (works numbers).
LZ61 (L21)	Zeppelin/Q	1916	1,359,435	585	61.3	4 Maybach (240)	58.9	Shot down off Lowestoft by British planes on 28.11.16.
LZ62 (L30)	Zeppelin/R	1916	1,950,112	649.4	78.4	6 Maybach (240)	63.8	Enlarged. Broken up in 1920.
LZ63 (LZ93)	Zeppelin/P	1916	1,126,389	536.2	61.3	4 Maybach (210)	60.1	Enlarged.
LZ64 (L22)	Zeppelin/Q	1916	1,359,435	585	61.3	4 Maybach (240)	58.9	Shot down by a British flying boat on 28.5.16.
LZ65 (LZ95)	Zeppelin/Q	1916	1,359,435	585	61.3	4 Maybach (240)	58.9	Enlarged.
LZ66 (L23)	Zeppelin/Q	1916	1,359,435	585	61.3	4 Maybach (240)	58.9	Shot down by a British plane on 21.8.17.
LZ67 (LZ97)	Zeppelin/Q	1916	1,359,435	585	61.3	4 Maybach (240)	58.9	—
LZ68 (LZ98)	Zeppelin/Q	1916	1,359,435	585	61.3	4 Maybach (240)	58.9	—
LZ69 (L24)	Zeppelin/Q	1916	1,359,435	585	61.3	4 Maybach (240)	58.9	Burned after breaking her back across the entrance of her shed.
LZ71 (LZ101)	Zeppelin/Q	1916	1,359,435	585	61.3	4 Maybach (240)	58.9	—
LZ72 (L31)	Zeppelin/R	1916	1,950,112	649.4	78.4	6 Maybach (240)	63.8	Shot down at Potters Bar by a British aircraft on 2.10.16.
LZ73 (LZ103)	Zeppelin/Q	1916	1,359,435	585	61.3	4 Maybach (240)	58.9	—
LZ74 (L32)	Zeppelin/R	1916	1,950,112	649.4	78.4	6 Maybach (240)	63.8	Shot down at Great Burstead on 24.9.16.
LZ75 (L37)	Zeppelin/R	1916	1,950,112	649.4	78.4	6 Maybach (240)	63.8	Broken up in 1920. Parts were sent to Japan.
LZ76 (L33)	Zeppelin/R	1916	1,950,112	649.4	78.4	6 Maybach (240)	63.8	Force landed at Little Wigborough on 24.9.16.

**These "P" class ships were enlarged to a volume of 1,264,100cu.ft. Length 585.5ft. and diameter 61.4ft. Powered by four 240hp Maybach engines. Maximum speed 60.1mph. No details available on other "P" class ships.*

GERMAN RIGID AIRSHIPS

Class/Name	Make/Type	Launched	Vol. (cu.ft.)	Dimensions (ft) Length	Diam.	Engines No.(hp each)	Speed max. mph	Remarks
LZ77 (LZ107)	Zeppelin/Q	1916	1,359,435	585	61.3	4 Maybach (240)	58.9	—
LZ78 (L34)	Zeppelin/R	1916	1,950,112	649.4	78.4	6 Maybach (240)	63.8	Shot down off Hartlepool on 27.10.16.
LZ79 (L41)	Zeppelin/R	1917	1,950,112	649.4	78.4	6 Maybach (240)	63.8	Wrecked by airship crews on 23.6.19.
LZ80 (L35)	Zeppelin/R	1916	1,950,112	649.4	78.4	6 Maybach (240)	63.8	Broken up on 15.10.18.
LZ81 (LZ111)	Zeppelin/Q	1916	1,359,435	585	61.3	4 Maybach (240)	58.9	—
LZ82 (L36)	Zeppelin/R	1916	1,950,112	649.4	78.4	6 Maybach (240)	63.8	Lost in forced landing on 7.2.17.
LZ83 (LZ111)	Zeppelin/R	1917	1,950,112	649.4	78.4	6 Maybach (240)	63.8	—
LZ84 (L38)	Zeppelin/R	1916	1,950,112	649.4	78.4	6 Maybach (240)	63.8	Forced landing in Russia on 29.12.16.
LZ85 (L45)	Zeppelin/R	1917	1,950,112	649.4	78.4	6 Maybach (240)	63.8	Forced landing in France on 20.10.17.
LZ86 (L39)	Zeppelin/R	1916	1,950,112	649.4	78.4	6 Maybach (240)	63.8	Shot down by AA fire over France on 17.3.17.
LZ87 (L47)	Zeppelin/R	1917	1,950,112	649.4	78.4	6 Maybach (240)	63.8	Destroyed in Alhorn explosion on 5.1.18.
LZ88 (L40)	Zeppelin/R	1917	1,950,112	649.4	78.4	6 Maybach (240)	63.8	Dismantled after crashing on 17.6.17.
LZ89 (L50)	Zeppelin/R	1917	1,950,112	649.4	78.4	6 Maybach (240)	63.8	Lost in Mediterranean on 20.10.17.
LZ90 (LZ120)	Zeppelin/R	1917	1,950,112	649.4	78.4	6 Maybach (240)	63.8	—
LZ91 (L42)	Zeppelin/S	1917	1,959,705	644.5	78.4	5 Maybach (240)	62	Enlarged. Sabotaged at Nordholz on 23.6.19.
LZ92 (L43)	Zeppelin/S	1917	1,959,705	644.5	78.4	5 Maybach (240)	62	Shot down over North Sea on 17.6.17 by a British plane.
LZ93 (L44)	Zeppelin/T	1917	1,970,298	644.5	78.4	5 Maybach (240)	64.4	Shot down by AA fire over France on 20.10.17.
LZ94 (L46)	Zeppelin/T	1917	1,970,298	644.5	78.4	5 Maybach (240)	64.4	Destroyed in Alhorn explosion on 5.1.18 with

Class/Name	Make/Type	Launched	Vol. (cu.ft.)	Dimensions (ft) Length	Diam.	Engines No.(hp each)	Speed max. mph	Remarks
								L47, 51, 58 and *SL20*. Crew saved.
LZ95 (L48)	Zeppelin/U	1917	1,970,298	644.5	78.4	5 Maybach (240)	66.9	Shot down over Suffolk on 17.6.17.
LZ96 (L49)	Zeppelin/U	1917	1,970,298	644.5	78.4	5 Maybach (250)	66.9	Forced landing in France on 20.10.17.
LZ97 (L51)	Zeppelin/U	1917	1,970,298	644.5	78.4	5 Maybach (240)	66.9	Destroyed in Alhorn explosion on 5.1.18.
LZ98 (L52)	Zeppelin/U	1917	1,970,298	644.5	78.4	5 Maybach (240)	66.9	Wrecked by airship crews on 9.10.18.
LZ99 (L54)	Zeppelin/U	1917	1,970,298	644.5	78.4	5 Maybach (240)	66.9	Destroyed by carrier strike from HMS *Furious* on 19.7.18.
LZ100 (L53)	Zeppelin/V	1917	1,977,360	644.5	78.4	5 Maybach (240)	74.4	Shot down by British aircraft on 11.10.18.
LZ101 (L55)	Zeppelin/V	1917	1,977,360	644.5	78.4	5 Maybach (240)	74.4	Lost in forced landing on 20.10.17.
LZ102 (L57)	Zeppelin/W	1917	2,418,350	742.9	78.4	5 Maybach (240)	63.8	Exploded in shed at Jüterborg on 7/8.10.17.
LZ103 (L56)	Zeppelin/V	1917	1,977,360	644.5	78.4	5 Maybach (240)	74.4	Wrecked by airship crews on 23.6.19.
LZ104 (L59)	Zeppelin/W	1917	2,418,350	742.9	78.4	5 Maybach (240)	63.8	"African" ship. Burned in air on 7.4.18.
LZ105 (L58)	Zeppelin/V	1917	1,977,360	644.5	78.4	5 Maybach (240)	74.4	Destroyed in Alhorn explosion on 5.1.18.
LZ106 (L61)	Zeppelin/V	1917	1,977,360	644.5	78.4	5 Maybach (240)	74.4	Surrendered to Italy on 29.8.20.
LZ107 (L62)	Zeppelin/V	1918	1,977,360	644.5	78.4	5 Maybach (240)	74.4	Exploded in air near Heligoland on 10.5.18.
LZ108 (L60)	Zeppelin/V	1917	1,977,360	644.5	78.4	5 Maybach (240)	74.4	Destroyed by carrier strike on 19.7.18.
LZ109 (L64)	Zeppelin/V	1918	1,977,360	644.5	78.4	5 Maybach (240)	74.4	Surrendered to England on 21.7.20.

GERMAN RIGID AIRSHIPS

Class/Name	Make/Type	Launched	Vol. (cu.ft.)	Dimensions (ft) Length	Diam.	Engines No.(hp each)	Speed max. mph	Remarks
LZ110 (L63)	Zeppelin/V	1918	1,977,360	644.5	78.4	5 Maybach (240)	74.4	Wrecked by airship crews on 23.6.19.
LZ111 (L65)	Zeppelin/V	1918	1,977,360	644.5	78.4	5 Maybach (240)	74.4	Wrecked by airship crews on 23.6.19.
LZ112 (L70)	Zeppelin/X	1918	2,196,282	693.7	78.4	7 Maybach (260)	80.6	Shot down off Norfolk coast 6/5.8.18.
LZ113 (L71)	Zeppelin/X	1918	2,196,282	693.7	78.4	6 Maybach (260)	72.7	Surrendered to England and broken up on 30.6.20.
LZ114 (L72)	Zeppelin/X	1920	2,418,700	743.2	78.4	6 Maybach (260)	72.7	Surrendered to France. Lost at sea with all crew on 21.12.23.
LZ120/Bodensee	Zeppelin	1919	700,000 (706,200?)	400 (396?)	61 (61.3?)	4 Maybach (260)	80 (81.2?)	DELAG ship. Sent to Italy in 1920. Broken up.
LZ121/Nordstern	Zeppelin	1921	794,700	—	—	—	—	Built for DELAG but taken over by France on 13.6.21. Deleted in 1926.
LZ126 (ZR3)/Los Angeles	Zeppelin	1924	2,471,700	656.6	90.5	5 Maybach (400)	68	Made for U.S. Government at Friedrichafen. Deleted in 1938.
LZ127/Graf Zeppelin I	Zeppelin	1928	3,700,000 (Blau gas vol. 1,226,080)	775	100 (Ht.113)	5 Maybach (550)	79.6 (Cruising 68)	Broken up in shed at Frankfurt in March 1940.
LZ129/Hindenburg	Zeppelin	1936	7,063,000	804	135 (Ht. 147)	4 Mercedes Benz diesels (1,200)	84.4 (Cruising 78)	Made 63 flights, out of which 37 were ocean crossings. Caught fire at Lakehurst N.J. on 6.5.37. 35 killed and 62 saved.
LZ130/Graf Zeppelin II	Zeppelin	1938	7,063,000	804	135 (Ht. 147)	4 Mercedes Benz diesels (1,200)	—	Last flight on 20.8.39. Broken up at Frankfurt, March 1940.
LZ132	Zeppelin	—	8,500,000	874	137.6	4 diesels (1,800)	Designed 100	Not completed. Designed to carry 42 tons of cargo or 100 passengers and 40 crew.

Willows Airships

The failure of Barton's airship in 1903 provided E. T. Willows with the fillip needed to produce a successful airship. His first airship was produced in collaboration with Captain William Beedle, who had constructed an airship of his own based on new ideas for deflecting the course of the ship. Beedle's first innovation was the regulation of the amount of air in compartments at each end of his ship so as to alter the angle of flight; alternatively sliding weights could be moved, or the car tilted to achieve this effect. The last method was by movable plane surfaces. These methods were largely unreliable and often impractical, but gave Willows a basis for a more precise system. Willows' idea was to alter the direction of the propeller thrust by swivelling the propeller through 180 degrees.

The first Willows airship was similar to Beedle's craft, and like the system used by Beedle, Willows had a propeller for propulsion distinct from the steering propellers, which were mounted on a pivoted carriage. The frame was triangular in section, with tapered ends. The envelope was made of Japanese silk and had a fineness ratio of 4 to 1. The ship was powered by a 7 h.p. Peugeot motor-cycle engine, with no silencer, and a length of flexible tube carried the exhaust fumes several feet below the platform. She was the first airship to fly heavy — about 40 lb.

Willows Airship No. 1 flew for the first time in 1905 and was a great success, being truly dirigible. It answered to its steering perfectly and could be turned completely round in its own length, albeit in calm weather. Willows went on to construct five more airships, each one incorporating substantial modifications, and he flew them all with varying degrees of success. These ships all had a rudder plane and a pair of swivelling propellers.

Willows' second airship had a 30 h.p. engine, and he made a flight

Spencer's airship *No. 1*

Dr Barton's semi-rigid airship

Willows 1 in June 1905

from Cardiff to London in 9 hours. This ship was followed by the *City of Cardiff*, which was a greater success. Willows made the first airship Channel crossing from England to the Continent in this little ship in about 13½ hours. Two more airships were built by 1913, the fourth being taken over by the Royal Navy in 1912.

The last ship built by Willows was constructed by Airships Ltd. and had the naval designation of *SS 2*. This airship was 70,000 cubic feet in capacity and was the largest airship designed by Willows. The ship

Willows 3

The car of *Willows 3*

Willows 4 became *Naval Airship No. 2* and after trials at Farnborough all control surfaces were removed from the boom and placed on the stern of the envelope

was powered by a 90 h.p. Curtiss engine, with an airship car and belt-driven swivelling propellers. The car was suspended from the envelope by wooden toggles attached to a rigging band. The stabilising system was one of the most complicated Willows ever designed: it had fins and planes arranged on the four sides of the envelope. Heavily doped aeroplane fabric was used for the envelope

The *Bournemouth* with her second set of (de Havilland) planes in 1952. On her first and second flights in 1951 she had a top plane which was later removed

The two-seater car and swivelling gear of the early *Willows 4* airship

Chitty Bang Bang

AD 1 photographed in 1930

as airship fabric was unobtainable, and although the swivelling gear worked well, the ship could only just reach a top speed of 36 m.p.h. therefore, it was rejected by the Admiralty as unsuitable, and this failure ended Willows' pioneering career in the airship field. His experiments over ten years with airships had bankrupted him, and it was while trying to earn a living as a fairground balloon operator in 1926 that he was killed when the envelope broke free.

Don Cameron's hot-air airship

Cameron D 96 Hot-Air Airship

The *D 96* is the world's first hot-air airship and was designed and produced by Cameron Balloons Ltd. as a sporting craft with commercial applications. The manufacturers of *D 96* also produce hot-air balloons ranging in volume from 20,000 cubic feet to 375,000 cubic feet.

The first flight of this airship was made at Wantage in Berkshire on 4 January 1973. At this time the airship had a single lower vertical stabiliser at the aft end, which provided only marginal directional stability, so a second, upper stabiliser was added. Since that time, an improved method of suspending the car has been evolved, thus eliminating the distortion of the envelope which occurred on the early tests.

The envelope is made from a light, high-strength nylon fabric. The lightweight tubular-metal gondola, which carried the propane burner, gas supply, pilot, passenger and power plant, was built by an engineering firm at Oxford.

The power plant is a modified 1,600 cc Volkswagen motor car engine, driving a large-diameter semi-shrouded pusher propeller. The endurance is about 2¼ hours.

Flight testing carried out since 1973 has suggested a number of improvements which will be incorporated in any production models.

Anthony Smith's Airship Santos-Dumont

The small non-rigid airship constructed by Mr A. Smith flew for the first time in May 1974 when inflated with hydrogen; in 1975 the craft was inflated with helium.

The envelope of this airship has a fineness ratio of 2 to 62, with ballonets fore and aft. Lightweight tubular structures are attached,

Anthony Smith's non-rigid airship *Santos Dumont*

Sky Ship being demonstrated in one of the hangars at Cardington

by patches, aft of the envelope, two of which, on either side of the centreline, carry fixed horizontal surfaces. Elevators are attached to the trailing-edges of these surfaces. Twin central surfaces are carried in a similar manner, a rudder being attached to the trailing-edges of these surfaces.

The car is also made of lightweight tubular material, and on its rear are mounted two 220 h.p. Wankel-type engines, each driving a small ducted propeller of the type used in small hovercraft. Airscoops for the inflation of the ballonets are mounted in the slipstream from the propellers. Fuel is contained in a single five-gallon tank, and 100 lb. of ballast is carried.

Sky Ship

A small group of business men together with John West Design Associates have set up a company to design a range of airships with payloads varying from 100 to 1,000 tons. This research and development company is known as Skyship Research and Development Ltd and will hold all patents and designs linked with the project. A second company known as Intercontinental Skyship (Transport) Ltd, was formed to develop the commercial aspect of the project.

After considerable research, the company considered that a disc-shaped vessel was the most feasible for their purposes. With the proposed symmetrical lenticular shape the Sky Ship would be 700 feet in diameter and the maximum thickness would be 208 feet. The structure of the ship together with all systems, ballast and engines would weigh 400 tons, while the disposable lift would be 400 tons also. This would give an all up weight of 800 tons. The Sky Ship would have a 70- to 90-knot cruising speed, with a maximum speed of 100 knots.

The cost of the vessel described above would be £10 to £15 million, with the eventual cost being determined by the selection of control systems and other sophisticated equipment.

A model of the 400-ton Sky Ship was demonstrated at Cardington in April 1975 and details of this model can be found in the table giving data on British private airships.

Early British Airships

Britain entered the field of military aerostatics in 1878 with the establishment of an Army Balloon Equipment store at Woolwich. In 1890 the store was moved to Aldershot and became part of the Royal Engineers. However, it was not until 1902 that the War Office finally allocated funds for the design of an airship at Farnborough. This project eventually ran out of funds and had to be shelved, and it was not until 1907 that more money was handed out by the authorities for the continuation of the project.

The result of the government cash injection was a renewed effort at Farnborough, which was epitomised in the labours of Colonel John Capper and Samuel Cody, who produced the *British Army Dirigible No. 1*. The ship, known as the *Nulli Secundus*, made its first flight at Farnborough on 10 September 1907. On 5 October Colonel Capper and Cody took the *Nulli Secundus* on a successful publicity flight to London, but because of bad weather the ship was marooned at the Crystal Palace for 5 days on its return journey, and had to be deflated and taken back to Farnborough by road.

Nulli Secundus was reconstructed in 1908, and in 1909 was followed by *Baby*, a smaller ship designed purely for experimental purposes, and modelled on the Clément-Bard ships of that date. Various power units were tried but she was difficult to control, and at the end of 1909 it was decided to lengthen her. She re-appeared in May 1910 as *Beta 1* and was in use sporadically until 1913, and even early in 1914 for mooring mast experiments. She was the first British

The semi-rigid British *Army Dirigible No. 1*, or *Nulli Secundus*, made her first flight on 10 September 1907. She was then modified with stabilising planes aft to check pitching, and made five flights. The photograph shows *No. 1*, after reconstruction, but without her car, before her first flight on 24 July 1908. The *Nulli Secundus,* also known as *Alpha,* then made three flights before she was deflated on 25 August 1908.

After making six flights the *Baby* was modified, and then five more flights were recorded, the last being on 23 December 1909

Gamma, Army Dirigible No. 3, landing in 1910. In March of that year the rudder was taken from the car and placed on the envelope

airship to be fitted with WT and the first non-rigid in the world to be moored out on a mast. *Nulli Secundus* was officially known as *Army Dirigible No.1*, and *Baby* was known as *No. 3*.

Gamma II enlarged to 101,000 cubic feet. The powerful box-kite elevator can be seen on the tail of the car

In February 1910 *No. 2* later known as *Gamma*, was launched. She was the first British Service ship to have swivelling propellers. In 1911 she was provided with two engines, and in 1912 E.T. Willows built a larger envelope. She was in use until July 1914, having proved to be a useful training ship.

In 1910 *Clément-Bayard 2* arrived at Wormwood Scrubbs from France, but her envelope leaked so badly that she was deflated and never flown. Soon after the Lebaudy *Morning Post* landed at Farnborough, but she was higher than originally planned, the shed was too low, and she was damaged and deflated while being docked. In May 1911 she was wrecked on her first flight at Farnborough.

Beta 1, the enlarged *Baby*, over Aldershot in 1910

Delta climbing vertically by using her swivelling propellers

Delta, intended to be a semi-rigid, was launched in September 1912, but the girders laced on each side of the envelope failed under the weight of the car, and in the end she was flown as a non-rigid. She was the fastest non-rigid of her day (44.5 m.p.h.), but was never very successful, except on the 1913 manoeuvres, when she took off 650 lb heavy, using her swivelling propellers. She was used at the Spithead review at the test mobilisation of the fleet in July 1914, but failed on patrol in August, and was deflated and not flown again. *Eta*, the last of the army airships, had her first flight in August 1913, and, except for problems with the chain drive to her swivelling propellers proved to be a useful ship until envelope trouble developed in the autumn of 1914, when an attempt was made to send her to Belgium, but she was so badly damaged while moored out in a gale in November 1914, that like *Delta*, she was deflated and stored away.

On 1 January 1914 all the Army airships were transferred to the Naval Wing of the RFC, but remained on station at Farnborough. These ships included *Beta II* which was a larger edition of Beta I, but with a boat-shaped car and a 50 h.p. Clerget engine. *Beta I* with 35 h.p. at her disposal could reach about 26 m.p.h., and *Beta II* some 36 m.p.h. *Beta II* was in use until 1915, having served in Belgium instead of *Eta*.

The car and swivel propellers of *Delta*

Eta 1 with enlarged bottom planes. She became *Naval Airship No. 20* in 1914

In September 1912 the Admiralty bought *Willows 4*, which then became *Naval Airship No. 2*. In 1913 she was given a larger envelope of some 39,000 cubic feet, and was then in use on and off as a school ship until June 1914. The original Willows car was then scrapped, and replaced by a new three-seater car with dual control, but only one flight was made with this car, and in March 1915 the envelope of 1913 was attached to a stripped down BE2c fuselage and became *SS 1*. This ship was the forerunner of the successful fleet of Submarine Scout airships which were used for anti-submarine and mine hunting duies.

In 1913, a French Astra-Torres, and a German Parseval were tested and became Naval airships *3* and *4*. In August 1914 these were the only British naval airships of real operational value, and were used to escort the original British Expeditionary Force to France, and also demonstrated the value of non-rigid airships for patrol duties. In 1915 *No. 8*, a larger Astra, was also employed to patrol the Channel, and much later in the war Parsevals *5* and *6* were commissioned into the Royal Naval Air Service (RNAS). Parseval *No. 7* was also delivered but was "cannibalised" and her parts were used as spares for the other Parsevals.

The Parseval *Naval Airship No. 5* with her enclosed Coastal-type car

The Parseval *Naval Airship No. 4*

The Astra-Torres *Naval Airship No. 3* on her first flight on 12 June 1913 at Kingsnorth

The semi-enclosed car of the modified *Naval Airship No. 4*

The SS ships were made by various firms, the parts being assembled mostly at Kingsnorth and Wormwood Scrubbs. The firm of Airships Ltd built twelve, and Armstrong Whitworth built nine, at least as far as the cars were concerned. By the end of the war 139 SS airships of various types had been built, in addition to the Parsevals, 32 Coastals, 10 C Stars and 16 North Sea ships, though some of the latter were reconstructions.

During the First World War 213 non-rigid airships were built for the Royal Navy, of which, thirteen were reconstructed. These ships achieved a remarkable service record. Suffering only minor losses, the airship service operated on patrol and convoy duties and succeeded in achieving a reputation comparable to the one earned by the U.S. Airship Service in the Second World War.

Morning Post, the Lebaudy-built airship wrecked at Farnborough on 4 May 1911

Gamma II, Naval Airship No. 18, at Fort Grange in June 1914

The Parseval *Naval Airship No. 6*. She was ordered from Germany before the war, but only the envelope was delivered, and so Vickers constructed the car from drawings in their possession, but used swivelling propellers and made a number of other modifications

C 23 escorting a British convoy

S.S.Z
77

The two 50 h.p. Chenu engines aboard the car of *Eta II*. Part of the control car is also visible

SSZ 77 at Kingsnorth in January 1919

The car of *SSZ 71* at Kingsnorth in August 1918

Beta II, Naval Airship No. 17, in December 1914

The car of *Eta II*, showing the swivel propellers

The Shorts standard type *SS BE 3*

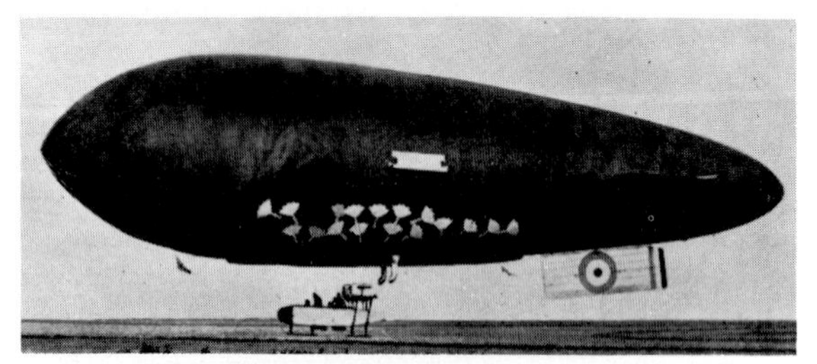

SST 2.Note the Eta patch suspension

Naval Airship No. 10, better known as *Eta II*

S.S T.I.

C ★1 in flight

SST 1 on the landing ground at Kingsnorth in September 1918

NS 16, the last of the "North Sea" class, was powered by two 260 h.p. Fiat engines

BRITISH PRIVATE AIRSHIPS

Class/Name	Make/Type	Launched	Vol. (cu.ft.)	Dimensions (ft) Length	Diam.	Engines No.(hp each)	Speed max. mph	Remarks
Spencer I/Mellin	Spencer-Moering (NR)	1902	30,000	93	24	1 Simms (3½)	—	Stanley Spencer was the first Englishman to build and fly a dirigible.
Spencer II	Spencer (NR)	1903	—	—	—	—	—	Larger than *Spencer I*. Envelope folded up on first flight. Afterwards used as free balloon without its engine.
Spencer No. 3	Spencer (NR)	—	40,000	84	32	1 Simms (5)	12.15	An exhibition airship. She was too slow and therefore only made a few flights. Gross lift 2,720lb.
Bovril	Spencer? (NR)	1914	—	—	—	1 Green (40-50)	—	Advertising ship for Bovril Ltd.
Barton	Barton (SR)	1905	227,396	169.9	27.2	2 Buchet (50)	15.5	Gross lift 8,172lb. Wrecked on her first flight from Alexandra Palace.
Willows 1	Willows (NR)	1905	12,000	74.1	18	1 Peugeot (7)	12	She had no elevators or rudder planes, therefore all directional control was by the inclination of the swivel propeller. The car was lengthened after the first flight in order to evenly distribute the weight. Gross lift 816.3lb.
Willows 2	Willows (NR)	1909	20,000	80	22	1 Jap (30)	18	Gross lift 1,360lb. Flew from Cardiff to London in 1910.
Willows 3/City of Cardiff	Willows (NR)	1910	33,000	110	26	1 Jap (35)	25	Fitted with swivel propellers. First airship to fly from London to Paris.
Willows 4/SS1	Willows (NR)	1912	20,000	90	20	1 Jap (35)	32	Gross lift 1,360lb. Became

BRITISH PRIVATE AIRSHIPS

Class/Name	Make/Type	Launched	Vol. (cu.ft.)	Dimensions (ft) Length	Diam.	Engines No.(hp each)	Speed max. mph	Remarks
						(Later Anzani)		*Naval Airship No. 2*. The first Farnborough modification was to remove all control surfaces from the boom and place them on the stern of the envelope. The envelope was enlarged to 39,000cu.ft. in 1913. Used as a school ship until June 1914. The original car was then scrapped with the exception of the swivel gear, which was used in a new three-seater car fitted with dual controls. See *SS1*.
Willows 5	Willows (NR)	1913	45,000	120	25	1 ENV (60)	35	Gross lift 3,060lb. Used as school ship 1913-14. Envelope trouble led to final deflation.
Willows 6/SS2	Airships Ltd. (NR)	1915	70,000	140	30	1 Curtiss (90)	36	Gross lift 4,760lb. Envelope made of doped aeroplane fabric. She made two flights at Kingsnorth. Designated *SS2* but because of her slow speed was not accepted as a service ship.
A.D.1	Airship Development Co. (NR)	1929	60,000	137.9	29 (width 38)	1 ABC Hornet later Rolls Royce (75)	50	Useful lift 15,000lb. with ABC engine and 12,000lb with Rolls Royce engine. Gross lift 4,250lb. approximately. Used for advertising around

Class/Name	Make/Type	Launched	Vol. (cu.ft.)	Dimensions (ft) Length	Diam.	Engines No.(hp each)	Speed max. mph	Remarks
								Newcastle. On her second inflation she flew to Dover and then to Belgium. She was deflated in a thunderstorm in August 1930, and then sent back to Britain and sold for scrap.
Bournemouth	Airship Club (NR)	1951	45,000	108	27 (height 45)	1 Salmson (60)	27	Gross lift 3,060lb. Useful lift approximately 13,000lb. The first set of planes were too small and made her unstable. In 1952 a larger set of planes were fitted which made the ship quite controllable. Only eight flights were made through lack of funds; the last being made on 16.8.52 — Battle of Britain Day.
Chitty Bang Bang	M. Brighton (SR)	1967	37,000	112	30 (width 30) (height 44)	1 Volkswagen (40)	—	Lebaudy replica made for the film "Chitty Chitty Bang Bang". She was difficult to control as the elevating planes had little effect. This was the first British airship to be inflated with helium.
Cameron I(D96)	Cameron Balloons Ltd (NR)	1973	96,000 to 100,000	100	46 (height 60)	1 Volkswagen (45)	17	The world's first hot-air airship. Turning radius at 11.5 mph is 100ft. Endurance approximately 2½ hours.

BRITISH PRIVATE AIRSHIPS

Class/Name	Make/Type	Launched	Vol. (cu.ft.)	Dimensions (ft) Length	Diam.	Engines No.(hp each)	Speed max. mph	Remarks
Gloster	Gloster (NR)	1974	25,000	82	25	2 Hirth F10-A1B (26)	—	Engines are four cylinder horizontally opposed air-cooled two-stroke. Has two ballonets.
Santos Dumont	A. Smith (NR)	1974	33,000	76	29	2 Wankel-Type (20)	30	Each engine drives a ducted propeller. She can be inflated with helium or hydrogen. The pressure height of this ship is approximately 6,000ft. Weight empty 1,060lb.
MTA Type B	Aerospace Developments (NR)	1976	162,000	164.5	48.7	2 Lotus 907 (150)	63.5	Building at Cardington. 8-seater. Two crew. Car made from g.r.p. and carbon fibre. Sold to Venezuela. Part of order for 22 craft.
Sky Ship	Skyship Research and Development Ltd (R)	1975	—	—	30	Electrically powered	—	A model demonstrated at Cardington. Helium-filled and flown under remote control, with trailing lanyards for manual reversion in case of difficulties. The model is 9ft 6in high at the centre, and has a payload of 40lb, which mainly consists of batteries and radio-control equipment. Gross lift is 215lb.

Class/Name	Make/Type	Launched	Vol. (cu.ft.)	Dimensions (ft) Length	Diam.	Engines No.(hp each)	Speed max. mph	Remarks
No.1/Nulli Secundus	Balloon Factory Farnborough (SR)	1907 (SR)	50,000	122	25	1 Antoinette (50)	16-18	*Army Dirigible No.1* had a combined fly-wheel and starting wheel. Stabilising plane fitted to check pitching.
No.1 reconstructed/ Alpha	Balloon Factory Farnborough (SR)	1908 (SR)	56,000	122	25	1 Antoinette (50)	22	Gross lift 3,740lb. Useful lift 800lb.
No.3/Baby	Balloon FF	1909	21,186	83.9	24.9	2 Buchet (30)	16	The first airship to have a ballonet.
No.3 reconstructed/ Baby	Balloon FF	1909	21,186	83.9	24.9	1 REP (30)	20	Car and control surfaces reconstructed.
Beta I/Ex-Baby	Balloon FF	1910	33,307	104	24.9	1 Green (35)	26	*Baby* enlarged and modified.
Beta II/NA No.17	Royal Aircraft Factory	1912	42,000	116	26	1 Clerget (50)	35	Became *NA No.17* in 1914. Weight 1,840lb.
No.2/Gamma	Balloon FF	1910	75,000	154	25	1 Green (80)	30	Rudder removed from the car to the envelope.
Gamma reconstructed	Army Aircraft Factory	1911	80,000	161-162	25	2 Iris (40)	32	Her propellers now swivelled through 360°.
Gamma II/NA No.18	Royal Aircraft Factory — Willows & Co.	1912	101,000	169	34	2 Iris (40)	30	Control surfaces modified in 1913. Weight 4,300lb.
Delta/NA No.19	Royal Aircraft Factory	1912	173,000	198	39	2 White & Poppe (100)	44.5	Useful lift 3,635lb. Weight 8,932lb. Control surfaces modified several times.
Eta I/NA No.20	Royal Aircraft Factory	1913	118,000	188	33	2 Chenu (80)	42	Weight empty 6,100lb. Gross lift 8,024lb. Useful lift 2,700lb.
Naval Airship No.2	Willows & Co.	1912	20,000	90	20	1 Anzani (35)	32	Ex *Willows 4*. Only made a few flights.
Naval Airship No.2	Willows & Co. (car) R.A.F. (envelope)	1913	39,000	110	26	1 Anzani (35)	25	*NA No.2* reconstructed.
Naval Airship No.2	Armstrong — Whitworth	1915	39,000	110	26	1 Renault (40)	—	Modified *No.2*. Only one flight made. Weight 1,745lb.

BRITISH NON-RIGID SERVICE AIRSHIPS

Class/Name	Make/Type	Launched	Vol. (cu.ft.)	Dimensions (ft) Length	Diam.	Engines No.(hp each)	Speed max. mph	Remarks
NA No.3/Astra-Torres	Astra Co. (Paris)	1913	229,450	248	46.5	2 Chenu (200)	51.1	Modified a number of times. Deflated and stored in 1915.
Naval Airship No.4	Parseval Co.	1913	300,125	275	49.2	2 Maybach (170)	37	Gross lift 20,409lb. Useful lift 6,174lb.
NA No.4 enlarged	Parseval Co.	1913	360,000	301	51	2 Maybach (170)	42	Above reconstructed. Covered car added. Deflated in 1917.
Naval Airship No.5	Parseval Co.	1917	364,000	312	57	2 Renault (240)	53	This ship had an enclosed "Coastal" type car. Used until 1918.
NA Nos. 6 and 7	Parseval Co.	1915-17	364,000	312	51	2 Wolseley Maybach (180)	42	Useful lift 7,052lb. Sister ships.
NA No.6 modified	Vickers/Admiralty	1918	364,000	301	51	2 Renault (240)	57-60	Useful lift 8,760lb. Reconstructed *No.6* of 1915.
NA No.8/Astra-Torres	Astra Co. (Paris)	1914	400,000	297	58	2 Chenu (240)	48	Had trouble with her internal suspension.
NA No.10/Eta II	Astra Co (car) Admiralty (envelope etc)	1916	140,000	—	—	2 Chenu (50)	39	Experimental ship. Made three flights.
NA No.17/Beta II	RAF (ex-Army)	1912	42,000(?)	116	26	1 Clerget (50)	35	Best altitude reached was 4,200ft.
NA No.18/Gamma II	RAF/Willows (ex-Army)	1914	101,000	169	34	2 Iris (40)	30	Modified in 1914.
NA No.19/Delta	RAF (ex-Army)	1914	173,000	198	39	2 White & Poppe (100)	44	Gross lift 11,764lb.
NA No.20/Eta I	RAF	1914	118,000	188	33	2 Chenu (80)	42	Wrecked while mooring at Dorking on 19.11.14.
SS (BE)	Admiralty	1915	60,000	143.5	27.9	1 Renault (70)	46-52	Prototype of SS series.
SS I (Submarine Scout)	Armstrong-Whitworth Airships Ltd.	1915	39,000	100	26	BE2C (70)	48	First of ASW series. Fifty projected. Weight 1,960lb.
SS2	Airships Ltd.	1915	70,000	140	42.4	1 Curtiss (90)	36	Willows' craft.
SS3-26, 48, 49	Airships Ltd	1915-16	60,000	143.5	27.9	BE2C 1 Renault (70)	48	Two ships transferred to France.

Class/Name	Make/Type	Launched	Vol. (cu.ft.)	Dimensions (ft) Length	Diam.	Engines No.(hp each)	Speed max. mph	Remarks
SS AW 27, 40-47	Admiralty and Armstrong-Whitworth	1915-16	70,000	143	30	1 Green or RR (100)	49.5	Useful lift 1,709lb. *SS45* sold to Italy. Weight 3,051lb.
SS MF 28-39	Admiralty	1915-16	60,000	143.5	27.9	1 RR or Renault (82)	45	Useful lift 1,347lb. Longest flight 29.20 hours.
SS P1-6	Admiralty	1917-18	70,000	143.4	30	1 Green or RR (75-100)	52.5	Single pusher propeller.
SS O, later SS Zero 1-71	Admiralty	1916-18	70,500	143.4	30	1 RR (75)	56	Useful lift. 1,344lb. Enclosed nacelle.
SST2/MT1	Admiralty	1918	85,000	146.4	35	2 RR (75)	60+	Became *SSE2*.
SST1-14	Admiralty	1918	100,900	165	35	2 RR (75)	57.5	SS craft were sometimes towed from the coast by RN ships in order to provide an extended range.
Cor Coastal C1	Astra Co. and Admiralty	1915	140,000	—	—	2 Sunbeam (150)	45+	An experimental craft.
C2-27	Admiralty	1915-17	170,000	195	37 (Height 52)	2 Sunbeam (150) others 1 Berliet-Ford (100)	47	Craft with Berliet-Ford engines also had one 200hp Renault aft. Weight 7,415lb.
C*1-10	Admiralty	1918	210,000	*1-3* 207 *4-10* 217	49.3	1 Berliet-Ford (110) 1 Fiat (260)	56	Improved coastal craft. Weight 5,330lb.
North Sea NS1-5	Admiralty	1917	360,000	262	56.9	2 RR (250)	57.5	Gross lift 23,313lb.
NS6-16	Admiralty	1918	360,000	262	56.9	2 Fiat (260)	58	Useful lift 7,154lb. *NS14* sold to U.S.A. NS 11-16 had cars different from those of earlier ships.

The *Mayfly* approaching her mooring position on Cavendish Dock, Barrow, on 22 May 1911. This was the first airship to be moored at a mast. She withstood wind gusts of up to 43m.p.h. while moored on the raft at Barrow

British Rigid Airships

In 1909 the Admiralty accepted a tender for the first British rigid airship from Vickers. This airship, known as the *Mayfly*, was allowed for in the Naval Estimates of 1909, £35,000 being set aside for her construction. The *Mayfly* was constructed by Vickers at Barrow-in-Furness, and was the first airship to be moored at a mast which was on a raft at Cavendish Dock, Barrow. The *Mayfly* withstood winds of up to 43 m.p.h., but broke her back against the door of her floating shed while being prepared for her first flight. The result was a total wreck. This accident shook official confidence in airships, but only for a short time.

The machine gun post on *No. 23* can just be seen on the top of the envelope towards the nose

The swivel propellers on the forward car of *No. 9*

No. 24 during mooring mast trials in 1919. Her first flight was on 28 October 1917

During the First World War construction work had been carried out, by Vickers, on the rigid airship *R 9*. This prototype was completed and fitted with swivel propellers driven by two 180 h.p. Maybach engines forward and aft, but modified later with one 250 h.p. engine aft. The airship was then delivered to the Naval Air Service in April 1917. Short Brothers were then asked by the Admiralty to build two similar airships, and the airships *R 31* and *R 32* were the result. These ships had a wooden framework similar to the German Schütte-Lanz airships. The *R 31* was damaged beyond repair in a rain storm and was sold as scrap for £200. However, the *R 32* remained in service until she was deleted in 1921, when the Airship Service was shut down. Towards the end of the war five more rigid airships were built. These were the *R 23*, *R 24* and the *R 25*, the other two being of the "23X" class and were designated *R 27* and *R 29*. These ships logged over 1,284 flying hours between them and were used for great deal of experimental work. The *R 24* and later the *R 26* in particular were used for mooring mast experiments.

After the First World War, ten rigid airships were on the cards for

R 27 of the "R 23X" class on her first flight on 8 June 1918

R 26 made her first flight on 21 March 1918, after which she logged over 197 hours flying time. She was used for three-wire mooring experiments at Pulham in 1919

No. 9 made her first flight on 17 November 1916. The two cars of this ship were connected by an enclosed keel

No. 25, like its predecessors *No. 23* and *No. 24*, was used mainly for training and experimental purposes

completion, and of these the *R 33* and *R 34* can be regarded as the most successful. During her life the *R 33* was used for a great deal of experimental work. the most exciting probably being the hook-up experiments carried out with a de Havilland Humming Bird and two Gloster Grebe fighters. The most important tasks of the *R 33* were undoubtedly in connection with the *R 100* and the *R 101* projects, and it is a great shame that she was not used considerably more as a flying test-bed. If she had been, the *R 101* might have been more airworthy than in fact she was. The *R 33* was eventually deleted in 1927 for reasons of economy.

The "R 23X" class airship *R 29* logged a total of 438 flying hours

R 80

The Vickers *R 80*, one of the last rigid airships to be laid down during the First World War, was, unlike her British predecessors, not based on the Zeppelin design. She was "designed" by Barnes Wallis, who bettered the Germans by the reduced fineness ratio, which gave the *R 80* a decided aerodynamic advantage over any Zeppelin airship. The *R 80* made her first flight in June 1920 and was used mainly for training American airship crews for *R 38*. The ship made her last flight in September 1921, and was afterwards kept in her hangar until she was broken up in 1925 as a government economy measure.

The skeletal framework of *R 31* in her shed at Cardington

R 31 made her first flight on 29 July 1918

R 29. The port swivel propeller can be clearly seen in this photograph of one of the cars

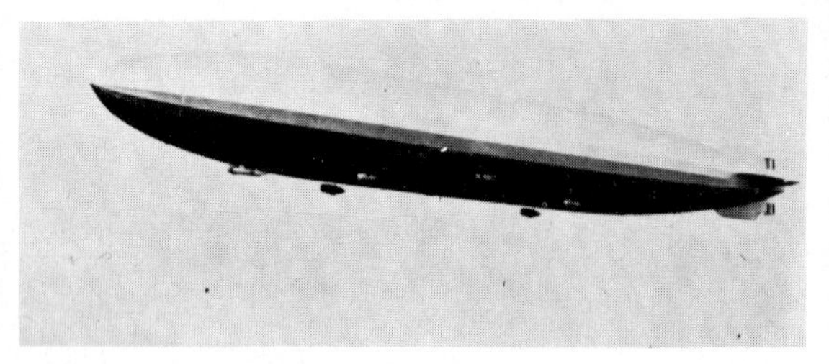

R 38 photographed in 1921

R 34 photographed while on her trip to America

R34

R.32

R 36 in flight over Cardington

The "R 31" class airship *R 32* photographed against a camouflaged wind-break at Cardington

R 33
R 33

R 80 made her first flight on 19 June 1920. During this flight she sustained damage to some of her girders. She was commissioned in 1921, and for a short time flew between Barrow and Howden. She then made four training flights for the U.S. Navy. She made her last flight on 20 September 1921

R 33 on the mast at Pulham

The 1924 Rigid Airship Programme

In 1924 the British Government initiated a research programme for the construction of large rigid airships for commercial operations. The end products of this project were the *R 100*, constructed by the Airship Guarantee Company, and the *R 101*, designed and built by the Air Ministry establishment at Cardington.

The airship built at Cardington was doomed to failure from the very start; its development was hampered by official interference, and the enormous publicity campaign which surrounded the project only forced the designers to incorporate even some of those aspects of their work which showed badly on trials. However, although a great deal of experimental work was carried out by the designers of the

R 100 on the mooring tower at Cardington

R 101, it is apparent that their work did not go far enough. Another contributory factor to the subsequent tragedy was that little exchange of information between the Cardington team and the designers of *R 100* took place. This failure to co-operate was largely the fault of the ingenuousness of Barnes Wallis, and, reportedly, the lack of tact of the people at Cardington. However it is only fair to mention that this lack of co-operation was mainly due to the bad organisation at top government level, but if an officer with the experience of the late Commandore Masterman had been in charge at Cardington, *R 101* would not have started on her flight for India before completing her trials.

R 100

The *R 100* was significant for the system of geodetic construction which was applied to it by Barnes Wallis. This ingenious principle of design was arrived at by sound theory and innumerable hours of calculations. The dictionary definition of geodetic can be quoted as "...the shortest possible line that can be drawn from one point of a surface to another, the plane of the curvature of which will be everywhere perpendicular to the surface". Nevil Shute, who was head of the calculating office at Howden and in part responsible for much of the work of the *R 100* describes the system proposed by Barnes Wallis in his autobiography *Slide Rule* as follows:

"..... each transverse frame consisted of a girder in the form of a stiff, sixteen-sided polygon with the flats at top and bottom; this girder was twenty-seven inches deep and up to a hundred and thirty feet in diameter. Sixteen steel cables ran from the centre of the polygon, the axis of the ship, to the corner points, bracing the polygonal girder against deflections. All loads, whether of gas lift, weights carried on the frame, or sheer wire reactions, were applied to the corner points of the polygon, and except in the case of the ship turning, these loads were symmetrical port and starboard. One half of the transverse frame, therefore, divided by a vertical plane passing through the axis of the ship, consisted of an *encastré* arched rib with ends free to slide towards each other, and this arched rib was braced by eight radial wires, some of which would go slack through the deflection of the arched rib under applied loads. Normally four or five wires would remain in tension, and for the first approximation the slack wires would be guessed. The forces and bending moments in the members could then be calculated by the solution of a lengthy simultaneous equation containing up to seven unknown quantities; this work usually occupied two calculators about a week, using a Fuller slide rule and working in pairs to check for arithmetical mistakes. In the solution it was usual to find a compression force in one or two of the radial wires; the whole process then had to be begun again using a different selection of wires.

"When a likely-looking solution had at last been obtained, deflecton diagrams were set out for the movements of the various corners of the polygon under the bending moments and loads found in the various portions of the arched rib, and these yielded the extension of the radial wires under load, which was compared with the calculated loads found in the wires. It was usual to find a discrepancy, perhaps due to arithmetical mistake by a tired calculator ten days before, and the calculations had to be repeated until this check was satisfied. When the deflections and the calculated loads agreed, it was not uncommon to discover that one of the wires thought to be slack, was, in fact, in tension as revealed by the deflection diagrams, which meant that the two calculators had to

moisten the lips and start again at the very beginning.

"The final check was to take vertical and horizontal components of the forces in every member of the frame to see that they equated to zero, that your pencil diagram was not sliding off the paper into the next room. When all forces were found to be in balance, and when all deflections proved to be in correspondence with the forces elongating the members, then we knew that we had reached the truth."

The girders of the *R 100* were formed of three duralumin tubes rolled up helically from sheetmetal and riveted with a helical seam. Transverse frames, polygonal rings made up of girders, were joined together by longitudinal girders, and the 15 gas bags, made of light fabric and lined with goldbeaters skin, were housed in the bays between the transverse frames. The framework of the airship was covered by an outer cover of linen fabric which was painted with aluminium dope. This outer cover was a weakness in both *R 100* and *R 101*. Relatively few longitudinal girders were used, which left larger unsupported panels of outer fabric than previous ships, which had incorporated many of these girders.

Six Rolls Royce Condor engines, aeroplane engines running on petrol, were installed in the *R 100*, two of which had reversing gearboxes to drive their propellers astern, to slow the ship down on her approach to the mooring mast. These Condor III B engines were placed in tandem in three cars, the rear engines being the reversible ones. A Bristol gas starter was installed in each car.

Electric power was supplied by 15 k.w. generators run by two AC 6-cylinder engines in the wing cars.

The 15 gas bags were made from one-ply cotton lined with goldbeaters skin, the largest of which (No. 7) had a capacity of 551,890 cubic feet.

R 100 under construction in her shed at Howden

A tail-view of the *R 100*

The fin length was 125 feet, extending from No. 12 frame to No. 15 frame, and the total fin area was 11,400 square feet.

The gross weight of the ship was 105 tons,and her disposable lift was 51 tons. Under standard conditions, with a gas purity of 95 per cent, her total lift was 156 long tons.

One of the features which distinguishes a rigid airship from an aeroplane is that every part is accessible and any repairs or maintenance that might be necessary can be carried out in flight. Should the wind hamper the work, the speed can be reduced to allow its continuation. Thus, when *R 100* made her flight to Canada, after extensive trials, she was on several occasions repaired in flight.

The *R 100* moored at St Hubert just 78 hours out from Cardington and stayed in Montreal for 12 days. She then made a local flight on which an engine failed. The return journey was made on five engines, but with the prevailing wind, and took 57½ hours.

This was the last flight the *R 100* made. On her return to Britain she was put into her shed at Cardington, and broken up and sold for scrap after the *R 101* disaster. When the *R 100* was demolished in 1931 the structure was reported to be in very good condition.

R 101

Barnes Wallis referred to the *R 101*, in recent correspondence, as the crudest piece of design he had ever seen, and mentions that it was also inferior to the framework of the *Naval Ship No. 1*, which had girders designed by the Works Manager at Barrow. However, it is interesting to note that Dr Ludwig Durr, the designer of the *Graf Zeppelin*, is quoted in Sir Peter Masefield's study of the *R 101* as saying that "I regard the R 101 as one of the best airships ever designed and constructed". The designers at Cardington may well have been ruled by the officials of the Air Ministry, who knew little of airships and were intent on gaining as much public support for the

The passenger deck of the *R 101* during construction

R 101 as the government's publicity machine could muster. However, it would be unfair to condemn the Cardington team as incompetent, for many of them were proved by their subsequent careers to be able and skilled men.

The rivalry between Cardington and Howden was perhaps the greatest contributory factor to the eventual disaster which befell the *R 101*, with, perhaps, the successful flight of the *R 100* to Canada taking second place. Moreover, the technical problems which beset the *R 101* were of the first magnitude, many of which, like the faulty valves and the chafing of the gas bags were not rectified before the ill-fated flight on 5 October 1930.

The ill-fated *R 101* on the tower at Cardington

To look at, the *R 101* was a magnificent piece of engineering, but under the veneer of sleekness were the mistakes which caused the deaths of some of Britain's finest airship men. The faults of the *R 101* are many and there is not enough space here to list them all, but the main ones can be considered to be as follows: that the design of the ship was misconceived, and that the construction was of poor standard. The materials used were not always of good quality, and the various installations, in particular the gas valves, were faulty and were never rectified. The ship was discovered to be dangerously overweight and a new bay was inserted in order to insert another gas bag to increase the useful lift. It was while work was being carried out on the new bay that the inadequacy of the padding around the gas bags was discovered and it was also noticed that they were literally being fouled by thousands of projections on the structure. This in itself was a product of bad design, for a system of transverse frames, triangular in section, was used in the *R 101*, in order to obviate the necessity for transverse bulkhead wiring; this lost 500,000 cubic feet that might otherwise have been used for lifting gas. This system of construction relied on a good clearance space between the hydrogen cells and the structure, and the girders were designed accordingly with nuts, bolts and the points of taper-pins protruding into the space. The consequence of this folly was that any movement of the gasbags brought them into contact with the structure so that holes and tears were made by the chafing. It is also worth mentioning that the outer cover of the *R 101* was strengthened in places by a system of tapes fixed to the interior of the ship with rubber solution. This adhesive reacted with the dope on the cover to make it very friable!

One of *R 101*'s gas bags inflated with hydrogen during her construction

R 101 slipped the mast at Cardington to make her flight to India at 6.36 p.m. on 4 October 1930. Many of those responsible for the ship were concerned about her state of airworthiness, and yet a temporary Certificate of Airworthiness was handed to her captain just before the flight began. However, by two o'clock the next morning the ship had only reached Beauvais, about 220 miles from her starting point; she was pitching and rolling a good deal and at about ten minutes past two she went into a steep dive. The *R 101* was brought out of this dive only to dive again a few moments later, when she hit the ground quite gently and burst into flames. Only six survived out of the fifty four persons on board. This was a high price to pay for government bungling and technical ignorance.

A public inquiry was held and the conclusions reached were that the disaster had been caused by a rent in the outer cover in the top forward region, which had exposed the gasbags to the violent airflow, and therefore the chafing and buffeting caused an enormous tear in the forward gas bag. The ship, as a result, lost height and on impact with the ground the escaping hydrogen exploded on mixing with the air or, perhaps, was ignited by a spark from a broken electrical circuit. There were other possible causes and therefore, in the final analysis, the decisions reached at the public inquiry cannot be taken as conclusive.

Thus the tragedy of the *R 101* heralded the end of rigid airships in Britain. Shortly after the inquiry the *R 100* was broken up and the frame, representing so much effort, was sold as scrap for £450. An ignominious exit for a superb airship.

Inside the control car of the *R 101*

Port and starboard views of one of the Beardsmore Tornado engines before installation on the *R 101*

Class/Name	Make/Type	Launched	Vol. (cu.ft.)	Dimensions (ft) Length	Diam.	Engines No.(hp each)	Speed max. mph	Remarks
No.1/Mayfly	Vickers	1911	663,518	512	48	2 Wolseley (80)	—	First British rigid airship. Wrecked during handling at Barrow. Weight 43,879lb.
No.9	Vickers	1916	889,310	520	53	2 W-Maybach (180) 1 Maybach (250) aft	45	Hours flown: 198.16. Engine data in the table is for

Class/Name	Make/Type	Launched	Vol. (cu.ft.)	Dimensions (ft) Length	Diam.	Engines No.(hp each)	Speed max. mph	Remarks
								1917-18. In 1916 she had four 180hp W-Maybach engines. Deleted in 1918.
No.23	Vickers	1917	942,000	535	53	4 Wolseley (250) Later 4 RR (250)	55	Hours flown: 321.30. Engine and swivel propeller configuration modified.
No.24	Vickers	1917	942,000	535	53	4 RR (250)	55	Hours flown: 164.12. The aft engine was taken out but put back at a later date. Used for mooring mast experiments.
No.25	Vickers	1917	942,000	535	53	4 RR (250)	55	Hours flown: 271.5. Two swivel propellers fore and two aft. Two fixed propellers midships. The gas bags surged badly.
R26 (No.26)	Vickers	1918	942,000	535	53	3 RR (200) and 1 Maybach (200)	55	Hours flown: 197.35. Completed on 20.3.18. Used for mooring experiments.
R27 (R23 X Class)	Admiralty	1918	990,000 (990,600?)	539	53	4 RR (250)	56.5	Approx. 90 hours flown. Burnt in shed on 16.8.18 at Howden due to fire started in an *SS Zero*.
R29 (R23 X Class)	Admiralty	1918	990,000	539	53	4 RR (250)	55	Hours flown: 438. Deleted 1920.
R31 (R31 Class)	Shorts	1918	1,553,000	614	65.5	6 later 5 RR (250-300)	65	Spent about 9 hours flying. The last flight was on 6.11.18. Deleted as dangerous owing to rotting of wooden framework in 1919.
R32 (R31 Class)	Shorts	1919	1,553,000	614	65.5	5 RR (250-300)	65	About 260 hours flying time. Deleted in 1921 on shutting

Class/Name	Make/Type	Launched	Vol. (cu.ft.)	Dimensions (ft) Length	Diam.	Engines No.(hp each)	Speed max. mph	Remarks
								down of Airship Service. Used as U.S.N. training ship.
R33	Armstrong-Whitworth	1919	1,950,000	643	78.9	5 Sunbeam (250)	62	About 800 hours flying time. Recommissioned, FF: 2.4.25. Broke away from mast during storm 16.4.25 and damaged. Repaired and used for experimental work. Although still in good flying order was deleted for reasons of economy in 1927.
R34	Beardmore	1919	1,950,000	643	89	5 Sunbeam (250)	62	About 500 hours flown. Broke up on landing ground in 1921 due to lack of mooring mast.
R36	Vickers	1921	2,101,000	672	78.9	2 Maybach (300) and 3 Sunbeam (323)	60	Made seven flights. About 80 hours flown. Overshot the mooring-mast at Pulham, causing severe damage, 21.6.21. Towed into shed and remained in her hangar until she was broken up in 1927. Weight 70,068lb.
R38	Shorts	1921	2,724,000	695	85.6 (height 931)	6 Cossack (350)	70.6	Broke in half and crashed in flames into the Humber on 24.8.21. The ship was known to be weak but trials were rushed due to the closing down of the Airship Service. 44 killed and five survivors. About 56.38

Class/Name	Make/Type	Launched	Vol. (cu.ft.)	Dimensions (ft) Length	Diam.	Engines No.(hp each)	Speed max. mph	Remarks
								hours flown. Weight 25,982lb.
R80	Vickers	1920	1,260,000	535	70	4 Wolseley-Maybach (230)	70	Hours flown about 73. Used for training American airship crews for a short time. Last flight 20.9.21. Dismantled in 1925 as an economy measure. Weight 52,416lb.
R100	Airship Guarantee Co. (a subsidiary of Vickers)	1929	5,000,000 (Total capacity 5,156,000)	709	130	6 Rolls Royce (700)	83	Fineness ratio 5½ to 1. Made nine flights, flying 297 hours. 827 hours spent at the mast. Made seven successful test flights and a return trip to Canada. Left Montreal 13.8.30. and landed at Cardington 16.8.30. This was her last flight. Deleted in 1930 and sold for £450 as scrap on 16.11.31. Weight 210,232lb.
R101	Air Ministry Establishment, Cardington	1929	5,000,000	722	132	5 Beardmore diesels (580)	72	Made twelve flights in 127 hours and 11 minutes. Started her last flight 4.9.30 and crashed on a hillside near Beauvais in France and burst into flames at 2.08 am the next day. Weight 250,400lb.
R101 Enlarged	Air Ministry Establishment, Cardington	1930	5,500,000	777	132	5 Beardmore diesels (580)	72	Modified *R101*. Weight 251,000lb.

Italian Airship Development

The Italian Government's interest in airships was aroused by French and German progress in airship design. From the beginning, the Italian designers favoured the semi-rigid type of construction. After a good deal of experimental work in which the first ships proved to be successful, regular construction of the "M" and "P" classes commenced. These ships were designed by Crocco and Ricaldoni, and were characterised by an efficient system of car suspension and envelopes of a good streamlined form. The envelopes were divided into a number of self-contained compartments, the purpose of which was two-fold: to prevent the entire loss of gas in the event of damage, and also to prevent the gas "surging". The latter is a tendency for the gas to collect at the highest end of the envelope, making it extremely difficult to resume an even keel.

This remarkable picture shows *F5* landing safely after sustaining severe damage in the course of action on 4 November 1918

Città di Milano was similar to *F1*, with a double envelope and the control car and engines incorporated in the keel

Of passing interest are the Usuelli designs, but the craft designed and used by General Umberto Nobile for the first air crossings of the North Pole were of a particularly good design. The first flight, in an airship, over the Pole was made in the *Norge*, the expedition being commanded by the Norwegian explorer Roald Amundsen. The second flight over this region was made in the *Italia*, under the command of Nobile. Unfortunately the ship was wrecked in tragic circumstances on the return journey.

Although the craft of the Italian Airship Service proved successful

A1, built in 1917, had a useful lift of 22,040lb

during the First World War, the tragedy which befell the *Italia* heralded the end of airship development in Italy. This incident prompted the Italian Government to accuse General Nobile, without justification, of neglect, and he then resigned from the army and went to Russia where he helped with the Russian airship construction programme.

The airships constructed by the Forlanini company differed somewhat from the government craft. The construction of the keel was different, being rigid inside the outer cover, hydrogen was contained in a number of compartments and the bags were enclosed within an outer cover. The air ballonet in the Forlanini ships was the space between the gasbags and the outer cover. The last Italian airship was the Forlanini *F7* which flew in 1931. This ship was mainly controlled by jet valves which were placed in the extreme bow and stern. The trials of *F7* were short but very promising, but were brought to a sudden end by the death of Signor Forlanini.

A close-up of the bombs carried on the side of an "A" class ship's car

N 2, the *Italia*, was lost after crossing the North Pole on 24 May 1928

Omnia Dir was manoeuvred by a unique omni-directional "jet control" system

The semi-rigid *MR* airship, constructed by the Stabilimento di Costruzioni Aeronautiche

M 1, the prototype of the "M" class

The improved "M" class ships *M 6* and *M 9* in a hangar at the Rome-Ciampino aerodrome. The machine gunner's position can be clearly seen on top of the envelope

A tavola non s'invecchia. The crew of the *M1* at luncheon. Major Leone is seated on the right, opposite Captain George Meager of the RNAS. The ship is just a few hours out from Ciampino over the Mediterranean

The Italian *T 34* was sold to America and appropriately renamed *Roma*. The ship was re-assembled in Virginia and on her maiden flight a fault in the elevator controls caused her to dive into high-tension cables with disastrous consequences

The car of *F 6*

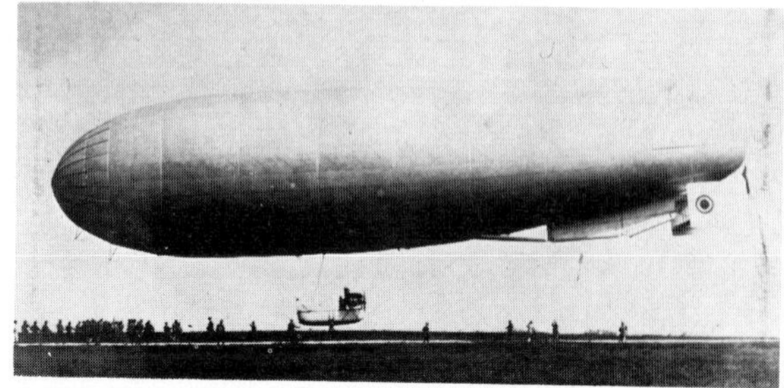

One of the "OS" or *Osservatore* ships landing at Ciampino

NORGE

SR 1, the Italian "M" class ship sold to Britain in 1918

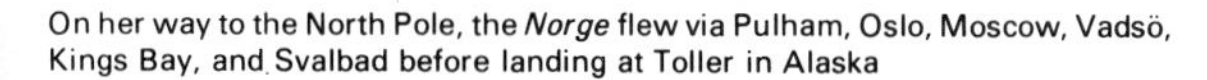

On her way to the North Pole, the *Norge* flew via Pulham, Oslo, Moscow, Vadsö, Kings Bay, and Svalbad before landing at Toller in Alaska

F 6, used as a military craft and also as a passenger ship

An Italian motorised kite-balloon

ITALIAN MILITARY AND PRIVATE AIRSHIPS

Class/Name	Make/Type	Launched	Vol. (cu.ft.)	Dimensions (ft) Length	Diam.	Engines No.(hp each)	Speed max. mph	Remarks
A1	SCA (SR)	1917	635,400	321.35	67 (width 63.97) (height 82.02)	4 SPA (225)	49.7	"A" class. Weight empty 18,960lb. Useful lift 22,040lb. Weight 22,050lb.
Ausonia	Nico Picolli (NR)	1909	63,558	137.10	(width 27.1)	1 SPA (40)	24.8	Damaged at Mantua while landing in a storm. Reconstructed.
Ausonia Bis	Nico Picolli (NR)	1910	52,965	121.5	(width 26.8)	1 SPA (55)	15	Reconstructed *Ausonia 1*. Deleted after being damaged in a storm.
1 Bis	SCA (SR)	1908	97,100	206.8	32.10	1 (100)	31	First Italian Army airship.
2 Bis	SCA (SR)	1909	123,585	229.8	34.8	1 (120)	32.9	Gross lift 84,034lb.
Italia I	Da Schio (NR)	1905	42,372	124.8	26.3	1 Buchet (12)	18.6	Given new motor. Reconstructed ship flew on 3.7.08. No ballonet. Damaged on 7.4.09.
Italia II	Da Schio (NR)	1913	91,806	164.1	34.5	1 SPA (50)	24.8	Gross lift 6,242lb. Designed by Count Almorico Da Schio.
DE	SCA (SR)	—	91,780	159.12	(width 34.45) (height 55.77)	1 Fiat A.10 (100)	40.30	ASW ship. Weight empty 6,305lb. Useful lift 1,782lb.
F.1/Leonardo da Vinci	Forlanini (SR)	1908	115,287	131.5	46 (width 45.1)	1 Antoinette (40)	31	Useful lift 1,684lb. Experimental ship. With internal keel and control car attached directly to the envelope.
F.2/Città di Milano (also Città di Ferrara)	Forlanini (SR)	1913	406,065	236.31	59.1	1 Isotta Fraschini (85)	39.1	Useful lift 9,800lb. Double envelope, and control car incorporated in the keel.
F.3	Forlanini (SR)	1915	530,000	295.3		4 Fiat (100)	45.9	Useful lift 21.000. Naval

ITALIAN MILITARY AND PRIVATE AIRSHIPS

Class/Name	Make/Type	Launched	Vol. (cu.ft.)	Dimensions (ft) Length	Diam.	Engines No.(hp each)	Speed max. mph	Remarks
					(width 59.1)			ship. *F3* and all subsequent "F" ships had an internal keel.
F.4	Forlanini (SR)	1916	487,140	295.2	59 (width 59.06) (height 82.02)	2 Isotta Fraschini (160)	44.64	Useful lift 11,396lb. Built for night bombing. Double envelope.
F.5	Forlanini (SR)	1917	635.400	295.29	(width 65.62) (height 88.58)	2 Isotta Fraschini (240)	46.5	Weight empty 21,384lb. Gross lift 4,3600lb. Useful lift 20,185lb. Army ship. Made 22 raids.
F.6	Forlanini (SR)	1918	618,440	295.29	(width 65.62) (height 88.58)	4 Isotta Fraschini (200)	62.14	Weight empty 21,825lb. Useful lift 19,261lb. Army ship. Used for passenger carrying after WWI.
F.7/Omnia Dir	Forlanini (SR)	1931	141,240	183.9	426	1 Isotta Fraschini (50)	—	This ship had an omni-directional "jet control" consisting of a blower in the keel and four valves on the bows and stern.
M.1	SCA (SR)	1912	441,375	271.3	55 (width 59) (height 89.08)	2 Fiat (250)	—	The *M* prototype ship.
M2-20	SCA (SR)	1915	441,250	264.04	(width 59.06) (height 89.08)	2 Itala D.1 (180)	42.17	Weight empty 18,077lb. Useful lift 10,890lb. Night bombing ships.
IM (1-?)	SCA (SR)	1916	441,250	269.04	(width 59.06)	2 Itala D.2 (220)	46.12	Weight empty 15,873lb. Useful lift 13,090lb.

Class/Name	Make/Type	Launched	Vol. (cu.ft.)	Dimensions (ft) Length	Diam.	Engines No.(hp each)	Speed max. mph	Remarks
					(height 86.29)			This class was built mainly for night bombing.
Naval M (NM) (1-?)	SCA (SR)	—	441,250	269	(width 59) (height 80)	4 SPA (250)	56	Used for ASW and long distance patrol duties.
MR	SCA (SR)	1924	35,885	105	25.6	1 Anzani (40)	40	Useful lift 990lb.
N1/Norge	SCA (SR)	1924	654,000	347.8	63.9	3 Maybach (250)	70.2	Weight empty 28,660lb. Useful lift 18,240lb. Flew over the North Pole on 12 May 1926. Dismantled at Toller in Alaska and did not fly again.
N2/Italia	SCA (SR)	1924	654,000	347.8	63.9	3 Maybach (250)	70.2	Weight empty 23,100lb. Useful lift 20,900b. Lost after crossing over the North Pole on 24 May 1928.
N3	SCA (SR)	1926	274,700	263	49	2 Maybach (245)	65	Useful lift 5,630lb. Sold to Japan. Became *NA No.6*.
O (1-?)	SCA (SR)	1918	123,700	177.8	35.4	— (240)	56.6	Weight empty 5,850lb. Gross lift 9,120lb. Useful lift 3,290lb.
O (with rigid stern) (1-?)	SCA (SR)	1921	123,700	177.8	35.4	— (240)	56.7	Modification of original "O" class with a rigid structure aft for her fins.
OS (1?)	SA (SR)	1918	176,000	222	44.5	2 (480)	53	Gross lift 12,560lb. Useful lift 5,500lb.
P1	SCA (SR)	1910	148,302	196.10	38.2	1 (105)	32.3	Gross lift 10,084lb. *P1* and *P2* made 91 operational flights against the Turks in the Tripoli War.
P2 and P3	SCA (SR)	1910	155,300	206.8	38.2	Clément-Bayard (120)	32.3	Gross lift 10,560lb. Deleted 1914.
P4-6	SCA (SR)	1912	176,500	203.42		2 Fiat-S54 (70)	40.30	Weight empty 8,377lb.

ITALIAN MILITARY AND PRIVATE AIRSHIPS

Class/Name	Make/Type	Launched	Vol. (cu.ft.)	Dimensions (ft) Length	Diam.	Engines No.(hp each)	Speed max. mph	Remarks
					(width 39.37) (height 70.54)			Useful lift 2,860lb. *P5* was named *Cittá da Jesi*.
P (Velocity)	SCA (SR)	—	176,500	203.42	(width 39.37) (height 70.54)	2 SPA (225)	55.92	Weight empty 8,267lb. Usefui lift 2,970lb. ASW and training craft.
Ricaldoni I and II	Crocco and Ricaldoni (?)	1909	—	216	36	1 Clément-Bayard (70)	27	A number of sister ships were apparently built.
SCA 1 and 2	SCA (SR)	1922	53,000	130	28	—	51	Weight empty 2,400lb. Bought by Spain.
SR1 (ex-M)	SCA (SR)	1918	441,250	269.04	(width 59.06) (height 86.29)	3 Itala & SPA (220)	51	Weight empty 15,873lb. Useful lift 13,090lb. Sold to the British Admiralty.
T.34/Roma	SCA (SR)	1919	1,204,000	410.1	74.6 (height 90.3)	6 Anseldo (500)	68.3	Gross lift 84,320lb. Useful lift 37,120lb. Sold to U.S.A. FF on 15.11.21. Crashed on 21.2.22. All U.S. ships were inflated with helium after this accident.
Usuelli	Usuelli and Borsalino (SR)	1910	135,000	167.4	(width 32.1)	1 P.A. (100)	31	Gross lift 1,378lb. Damaged in 1913.
Usuelli	Usuelli (SR)	—	141,200	180.4	(width 36.09) (height 54.13)	2 Fiat Colombo (100)	45.88	Weight empty 4,850lb. Useful lift 4,136lb. ASW craft.
AP-MB	Motorised AP (KB)	—	40,357	75.5	37.6	1 Anzani (40)	22.25	Motorised kite balloons.
V1-2	SCA (SR)	1915	553,210	287.08	(width 62.34) (height 85.3)	4 Itala D1 (180)	50.94	Weight empty 26,014lb. Ueful lift 12,532lb. Night bombing ships. *V1* was lost in 1915.

JAPAN

Private Airships

In April 1909, Mr Hamilton, an Englishman, demonstrated a small airship in Japan, and soon after a Provisional Military Balloon Research Society was formed, and an airship station erected at Tokorosawa on 30 July 1909. A Parseval airship was ordered from Germany and the firm of Yamada built airship *No.1*, a ship similar to Hamilton's craft. She was wrecked on landing after her first flight on 9 September 1910. *Yamada 2* was then built and after a few mishaps she exploded after a crash landing. Yamada then built a third and much more successful ship which was eventually sold to China.

Japanese Military Airships

The Japanese Army operated three airships in all; the last was flown until July 1917. Soon after the last army airship was phased out, the Japanese Navy took over airship operations. *No.1*, a Vickers SS Twin, the first naval airship, caught fire and was destroyed in her shed on 10 July 1922. This inauspicious start to the service did not deter the Japanese from building more airships and a total of nine craft flew in the service with great success. The last naval airship, *No.9*, a "Twin", was used until the Naval Airship Service was disbanded in 1933.

Flying Submarine Model 503

A group of Japan Experimental Aircraft Association members, led by Mr. Daisaku Okamoto and Mr. Kikuo Koizumi, has built a remotely controlled pilotless research airship preparatory to the construction of a large craft capable of carrying a pilot. An unusual feature of the design is the addition of a horizontal lifting surface attached to the lower structure of the car. This has a fixed centre section and movable outer panels to assist with vertical control as well as to provide lift.

The Japanese *Naval Airship No. 1* on a Vickers Masterman mast

Hamada II, a non-rigid Japanese airship which was first flown in February 1911

Orient Lease Company

The *WDL 1* airship manufactured in Germany at the WDL airship works in Essen-Mülheim, was sold to the Orient Lease Co. Ltd. of Tokyo and is operated by them in Japan. This ship made its first flight in October 1972 bearing the German serial No. 101. For technical data on this craft see under German non-rigid airships.

Prior to the sale of *WDL 1*, the old *Schwab* airship was sold to Japan, but was deleted after her mooring mast collapsed in a gale.

The Japan Experimental Aircraft Association's remotely controlled research airship, fitted with horizontal lifting surfaces

JAPANESE MILITARY AND EXPERIMENTAL AIRSHIPS

Class/Name	Make/Type	Launched	Vol. (cu.ft.)	Dimensions (ft) Length	Diam.	Engines No.(hp each)	Speed max. mph	Remarks
Yamada I	Yamada (NR)	1910	56,550	—	—	1 (automobile) (14)	—	Gross lift 3,845.4lb. Wrecked on landing after her first flight.
Yamada II	Yamada (NR)	1911	53,000	108	—	1 (50)	—	Gross lift 3,604lb. Had a number of mishaps when tested.
Yamada III	Yamada (NR)	—	35,320	127.6	(width 31.02)	—	—	Gross lift 2,381.7lb. Converted to a kite-balloon.
No.1 (Army)	Yamada and Heraka (NR)	1911	103,500	158.7	37	1 Wolseley (60)	—	Gross lift 7,100lb. Successful army training ship.
PL 13 (Army)	Parseval (NR)	1912	282,480	259.2	47.6	2 Maybach (150)	41.2	Gross lift 19,203lb. Useful lift 4,840lb. Army ship damaged in 1913. Enlarged.
Yuhi (reconstructed PL13)	— (NR)	1915	353,400	279	51 (height 74)	2 Maybach (150)	42.5	Gross lift 24,031.2lb. Last army airship. Flown until 1917.
No.1 (Naval)	Vickers Twin (NR)	1922	100,000	170.7	(width 36) (height 50)	2 Sunbeam Dyaks (100)	60+	Naval ship. Caught fire and destroyed soon after launch on 10.7.22.
No.2 (Naval)	Astra-Torres (NR)	1923	364,000	262.5	54 (height 71)	2 Sunbeam (300)	48	Took part in the Grand Naval Review of October 1924. Deleted soon after.
No.3 (Naval)	Navy Yard (NR)	1923	100,000	170.7	36	2 Rolls Royce (90)	60+	Exploded 1924 killing crew of five.
No.4 (Naval)	Navy Yard (NR)	—	111,500	182	—	2 Sunbeam (100)	55	Similar to British *SS Twins* of 1918. Remained in service until 1932.
Nos 5 and 9 (Naval)	Navy Yard (NR)	—	123,700	177	38.5 (height 54.5)	2 Benz (130)	56.5	Successful ships, in use until 1932.
No.6 (Naval)	SCA (SR)	1929	274,700	263	49 (height 59)	2 Maybach (245)	65	Built in Rome. First flight in Japan 6.4.27.

JAPANESE MILITARY AND EXPERIMENTAL AIRSHIPS

Class/Name	Make/Type	Launched	Vol. (cu.ft.)	Dimensions (ft) Length	Diam.	Engines No.(hp each)	Speed max. mph	Remarks
No.8 (Naval)	SCA (SR)	—	274,700	263	49	2 WC (150)	62	Destroyed in storm 1927. Useful lift 5,630lb. Used until 1952 when Naval Airships were disbanded.
Flying Submarine Model 503	JEAA (NR)	1975	—	25.7	—	2 4.99cc (0.63)	12.5	A remotely controlled research airship. Wing span 4ft. 1½in. Gross area of wing 9.47sq.ft. Gross weight 41lb. Ceiling 3,280ft.

Ljebedy, ex-*La Russie*

RUSSIA

Russian Airship Development

Up to the Russian Revolution it was the Imperial Russian Army which sponsored nearly all the recorded airship activity. From 1909 to August 1914, six Russian designed airships were built, and two more were constructed from designs based on Lebaudy and Zodiac ships. In addition to these a number of foreign airships were ordered. *Clément Bayard 1*, really *Astra 4* as the aerostatic part of the ship was built by Astra of Paris in 1908, was delivered and renamed *Berkout*. Then in 1913 *Clément Bayard 5*, sister ship to the famous *Adjutant Vincenot,* and *Depuy de Lôme,* was delivered.

In 1917, *Clément Bayard VII*, the Grand Cruiser *Général Meusnier* crashed on coming down from an altitude test in France on 7 April 1917, she did not fly again and was never delivered.

Astra XIII was sold to Russia in 1913, and in 1909 a semi-rigid Lebaudy airship was taken over and named *Ljebedj*. A second and larger Lebaudy, named *Kretchet*, was built in Russia in 1911, and in November and December of that year two small Zodiac *Vedettes* were tested in Russia and taken over and named *Tchaika* and *Korchoune*. *Le Temps*, the French newspaper presented *Korchoune* to Russia. Then in 1913, the German *Parseval 14* was bought and renamed *Griff*.

Little has come to light with regard to the fate of these ships, though in the early months of the First World War occasional references were made about raids carried out by Russian military airships.

In 1916 three British Coastal airships were bought for the Russian Navy, and it has been said that their shed was built so near to their pressure height that the ships could hardly be used. In any case the Revolution brought all airship activity to an end for some time.

General Nobile's departure in disgrace from Italy provided the Soviet Government with an airship designer of great skill, who was

The Russian Astra airship

Albatross, the third Russian Army airship to be constructed at the Ijora Aircraft Works

prepared to give his services to the evolution of Russian airships. About that time a "public subscription of 15 million roubles" towards a "Red Airship Programme" was announced, and it can be safely assumed that most of this money was spent on the nine or so semi-rigid airships of Nobile's design which were built and successfully flown by the Russians. Having contributed greatly towards Soviet airship development, General Nobile returned to Italy.

In 1933 plans to build two large airships, one at Leningrad and the other at Dalgo Prutnaya, near Moscow, were announced. Plans for a metal-clad airship were made public at the same time but nothing came of this project. In 1937 work began on a new semi-rigid airship, designed for Arctic research, and later that year the *V6* claimed an endurance record of 130 hours and 26 minutes flying time, exceeding the duration record previously held by the *Graf Zeppelin* in 1935, by eleven hours. The *V6* crashed two years later, and a passenger airship, built in 1934, crashed on a special trial flight on 6 February 1938. Although these accidents effectively put a stop to the production of large airships, the Russians were still operating the *V12* in the summer of 1945. The Russians reported the *V12* deleted in this year but the U.S. Navy has evidence to substantiate the existence of this airship in 1947.

Intermittent activity took place until early in the 1960s when a concerted effort by a few groups of airship enthusiasts resulted in the appearance of a small number of non-rigid craft and a handful of motorised kite-balloons. Since then a number of grandiose schemes have been promulgated, but the only project reported to have reached fruition is the strange *D1* airship.

A Soviet non-rigid airship prior to its first flight in 1931. About fifty similar craft were constructed for military and civil purposes between 1925 and 1940

D1

Work on the *D1* was carried out in Kiev by a design group headed by Roman Gokham. Construction and test flights were completed in 1969, and according to Soviet press reports, "were so successful that work began on a larger version" of the craft. There have been no reports of this project being completed.

It is claimed that the *D1* has a rigid body composed of a three-layer envelope made of glass-fibre laminates, the spaces between the layers being filled with expanded polystyrene foam. The skeletal framework, which is covered by this unusual envelope is made up of four transverse frames and four stringers. One of the stringers is reinforced to function as a corridor between the cabins, which are located in the bow, tail and centre of the craft.

The *D1* is powered by a turbofan engine mounted aft, and directional control is obtained by a set of rudders placed on the fin on the tail. Helium is used to inflate the 21 gas cells, which are made of thin synthetic material, and an automatic pressurisation system has been evolved to control lift.

The double-skinned semi-monocoque hull is impermeable to rain and frost; this, and the airship's special de-icing equipment, are stated to permit operations in nearly all types of weather. A tricycle undercarriage simplifies landing procedures and a low-level rotary mooring system was developed and used until a conventional mooring mast was available.

The maximum operating altitude of the *D1* is 22,965 feet and her range, at operational speeds of 105 to 124 m.p.h., is 1,864 miles.

The Soviet semi-rigid airship *V 6*, built in 1934. As the ship was not circular in cross section, the average diameter was 61 feet. The five double circumferential bands seen in the illustration are the locations of the five transverse diaphragms which divide the hull into six compartments

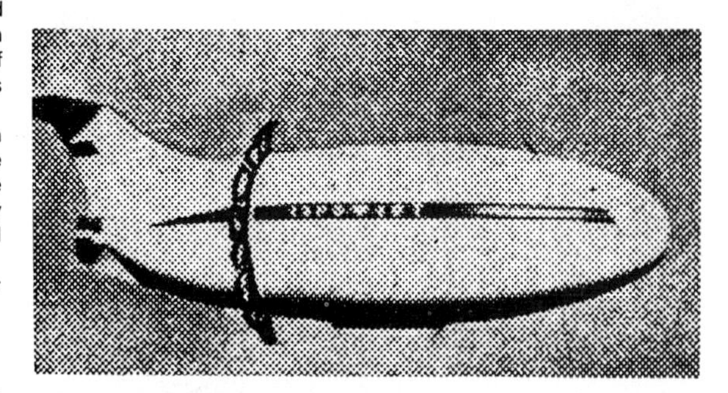

D-1, built in Kiev in 1969. This ship was to be the prototype for a series of ultra-modern rigid craft

Future Soviet Projects

Kite-balloons, tethered to and travelling along a capable system, are currently in use for the haulage of timber, and it is for this type of

C-OI

operation and as heavy-duty cranes for major construction projects, that the main interest in airship development appears to be centred in the Soviet Union.

It has also been reported that work is being carried out to evolve a lift control system that would eliminate the ballasting and costly valving routine that has been a conventional part of airship operations to date. This control system is envisaged as a means of heating and cooling the helium gas, so expanding or contracting the gas volume to regulate the lift. Successful development of such a system would enhance the economics of large-scale airship operations for the transport of heavy cargo and possibly passengers. It has been prophesied that large rigid airships will once again grace the skies, and in the not-too-distant future at that.

RUSSIAN AIRSHIPS

Class/Name	Make/Type	Launched	Vol. (cu.ft.)	Dimensions (ft) Length	Diam.	Engines No.(hp each)	Speed max. mph	Remarks
PL7/Griff	Parseval (NR)	1910	268,900	236.1	46	2 NAG (110)	36.7	Russian Army ship. Useful lift 4,840lb.
Astra XIII	Astra (NR)	1913	370,755	255.11	47.5	2 Chenu (100)	—	Sold to Russian Army 1914. Originally intended for passenger carrying as *Trans Aerienne II*.
Outchebny	Army Airship Works (NR)	1908	63,576	—	—	1 Vivinus (50)	21.5	School ship designed by Capt. A. Chabsky.
Ljebedy (ex La Russie)	Lebaudy (SR)	1908	128,000	203.5	36	1 Panhard (70)	—	Bought by the Russian Army from France.
Krechet (Falcon)	Army Airship Works/ Lebaudy (SR)	1911	201,195	229.8	45.11	2 Panhard-Levassor (100)	31	Gross lift 13,681lb. Second Russian Army airship (*No.2*).
Clément-Bayard 1/ Kommissiony	Astra and CB (NR)	1908	123,585	189.9	34.2	1 Clément-Bayard (116)	29.8	Made twenty ascents then sold to Russia after landing in the Seine.
Clément-Bayard 5	Clément-Bayard (NR)	1913	346,038	287	44.28	2 Clément-Bayard (120)	32	Sister ship to *Adjudant Vincenot* and *Dupuy de Lôme*.

This small non-rigid airship, photographed in 1965, is moored to what appears to be a forestry look-out tower. Craft of this type are known to be employed by the Soviet forestry authorities

RUSSIAN AIRSHIPS

Class/Name	Make/Type	Launched	Vol. (cu.ft.)	Dimensions (ft) Length	Diam.	Engines No.(hp each)	Speed max. mph	Remarks
Yastreb and Goloubj	Doux 1 (NR)	1910	86,300	165	42.9	1 Dansette Gillet (70)	—	Russian army airship. Gross lift 5,868.4lb.
Kobtechik	Duflour and Constantinovitch (NR)	1912	60,000	158.4	—	2 (45)	—	Modified Zodiac of the Russian Army.
Forszmann I	Forszmann (NR)	1910	28,256	122.1	(width 19.8)	1 Körting (40)	22.8	Gross lift 1,804lb. Built for Russian army.
Forszmann II	Forszmann (NR)	1911	21,192	115.5	(width 19.8)	1 Körting (25)	21.5	A one-man ship.
Golub	Ijora Aircraft Works (NR)	1910	78,176	151.8	(width 31.3)	1 Körting (75)	31	Army ship.
Sokol	Ijora Aircraft Works (NR)	1911	86,300	165	(width 33.3)	1 DeDion-Bouton (80)	33.5	Army ship. Gross lift 5,808lb.
Albatross and Condor	Ijora Aircraft Works (NR)	1914	282,560	—	—	2 Körting (150)	37.5	Army ship. Gross lift 19,200lb.
Kostevitch	— (NR)	1908	—	—	—	—	—	No other details available.
PL14	Parseval (NR)	1913	353,100	278.8	53.5	2 Maybach (180)	41.4	Bought for the army in 1913.
Gigant (Giant)	A.I. Shabsky (SR)	—	700,000	—	—	—	—	No other details available.
Tchäika and Korchouno	Zodiac (8 & 9) (NR)	1910	75,000	157.6	32.10	1 Labor & Dansette-Gillet (60)	24.8	Trials conducted by Count de la Vaulk in Russia.
V6 (B6)/Osoaviakhim (V1-V5?)	Nobile design (SR)	1934	685,000	349.5	61	3 Osoaviakhim (265)	—	*V6* was similar to the Italian *N* airships. This may have been the passenger ship reported to have crashed in 1936.
DP9	Dirigible Construction Trust (SR)	1936(?)	882,829	353	(height 79)	—	—	Passenger ship. Constructed 1936.
Klim Voroshiloff	DCT (SR)	1936(?)	779,922	341.2	82	—	62	—
Linin, Pravda, Kolchoznik, Stary Bolshevik, Komsomolez, Profintern	DCT (SR)	1936-38	1,901,306	492.1	—	—	—	With *Klim Vorishiloff* these airships formed the seven craft projected in the 1934-35 programme. Figures refer to second of class only.

Class/Name	Make/Type	Launched	Vol. (cu.ft.)	Dimensions (ft) Length	Diam.	Engines No.(hp each)	Speed max. mph	Remarks
V12 (B12)	DCT (SR)	1938	670,978	—	—	—	—	Still flying in July 1945.
Scouts (about 50 built)	— (NR)	1925-40	353,146	—	—	—	—	Successful class of ships. Four built in 1935.
Liningradsky Lesnichy (LL1)	— (NR)	1964	—	165	49.6	2	62	Designed in 1962 by V Murytshev and O. Antonov for forestry work. Crew: 5.
Ural 1	David Bimbat (NR)	1964	—	—	—	1 (?)	—	Used for filming, but designed for operation in remote areas.
Izvestia	David Bimbat (NR)	1964-65	—	—	—	—	—	Used for filming.
Bimbat	David Bimbat (NR)	1965	—	82	26.3	—	—	Used by Soviet film studios.
Novosibirsk 1	— (NR)	—	211,888	180.4	39.4	1 or 2	—	Designs of 1965. Not
Novosibirsk 2	— (SR)	—	2,472,026	505.25	118.1	2	137	reported as built.
D-1	Kiev Design Bureau (R)	1969	953,495	275.6	82	1 turboprop	124	Hull of semi-monocoque construction.

SPAIN

Torres Quevedo

The tri-lobe design of the Spanish *Torres Quevedo* airship of 1907 was highly successful and was subsequently adopted by the Astra firm of Paris who used it to great advantage in their line of Astra-Torres airships. These ships were later used for military purposes in France and England. The Astra-Torres ships were constructed at the Astra factory at Billancourt in Paris and at the sheds in Pau, Meaux, Rheims and Issy-les-Moulineaux, which enabled about six craft to be produced at the same time.

Reina Maria Cristina

The *Reina Maria Cristina* designed about 1930 by Commandante Maldonado and Captain F. Martinez was another exceptional Spanish airship. The latter designer had trained and qualified as an airship pilot with the U.S. Army. Although the airship was semi-rigid she has much in common with the American "TC" ships.

Automatic relief valves were placed in each side of the envelope and were controlled from the gondola. The ship had two ballonets, and the nose was stiffened by a structure of radiating ash ribs. The car was suspended by ropes attached to patches on the envelope. Three stabilising surfaces were attached to the envelope and there were also two horizontal planes with elevators, a fin and a rudder suspended beneath the tail.

The car was streamlined and was 26 feet 2½ inches long, 4 feet 11 inches wide and 6 feet 1 inch deep. The structure of this was of a four-ply wood covering on ash frames, stiffened with steel plates. The cockpit was open with seating for two, and there was accommodation for a mechanic and two passengers aft.

The two Walter radial engines were air-cooled and drove tractor airscrews. The engines were carried by outriggers of the aerofoil section on each side of the gondola.

SPANISH MILITARY AIRSHIPS

Class/Name	Make/Type	Launched	Vol.. (cu.ft.)	Dimensions (ft) Length	Diam.	Engines No.(hp each)	Speed max. mph	Remarks
Torres Quevedo	Torres (NR)	1907	33,907	118.8	(width 19.6)	1 (48)	—	The first Torres tri-lobe airship. Design taken over by Astra.
Espana	Astra (NR)	1909	148,307	213.3	37	1 Panhard (110)	27.9	The first Spanish military ship. Ascent made by the King of Spain.
Alfonso XIII	Torres Quevedo (NR)	—	—	—	—	—	—	Destroyed by an explosion on 10.8.15.
SCA 1 and 2	SCA	1922	53,000	130	28	—	51	Flown from a carrier in the Morroccan Campaign.
Reina Maria Cristina	Spanish Army (SR) Armament Works	1930(?)	142,200	177	39.5	2 Walter (120)	56	Training and experimental ship.

Goodyear Airship Operation

Since 1917 the American company of Goodyear has built a total of 301 airships, more than any other company in the world. Of these, 244 were constructed under contract for the US Army and Navy, and include the USS *Akron* and USS *Macon*, the largest rigid airships constructed in the U.S.A. The remainder have been commercial airships, of which the first was the *Pilgrim*, launched in 1925, and inflated with helium, as were all Goodyear airships built after that time.

In 1916 the U.S. Navy began a non-rigid airship development plan. At first it was intended to produce a small ship for experimental purposes, but by 1917 the prospect of U.S. involvement in the war in Europe prompted the Navy to order sixteen airships. These ships were to be known as the "B" class and were intended for training airship crews and for ASW purposes. Nine of the class were ordered from Goodyear, the last being completed and delivered by March 1918. The remaining seven airships were built by the B.F. Goodrich Company and the Connecticut Aircraft Company. A contract to build the navy-designed *A1* (*DN1*) was awarded to the latter company in 1915 but this airship was not completed until 1917. The *A1* was a partial failure and all subsequent contracts for non rigid-airships were awarded to Goodyear.

An advanced airship design was next on the agenda. This type of airship, known as the "C" class, was powered by two 150 h.p. Hispano Suiza engines and had a speed of 60 m.p.h., and an increased range. The first of the "C" airships carried a Curtise biplane to a height of 2,500 feet and released it in mid-flight.

In the 1920s Goodyear built a large number of non-rigid airships for commercial purposes and experimental work, and it is thanks to this commercial exploitation of airships that the U.S. Navy was able to operate a force of patrol airships during the Second World War.

Volunteer. On her first flight on 27 April 1929 she had a capacity of 86,000 cubic feet, but in January 1931 the envelope was enlarged to 96,000 cubic feet

The car of *Enterprise 1* with both Warner 145h.p., direct-drive engines visible

This is made plainly clear by the fact that the U.S. Navy Airship Service mainly consisted of a few obsolete types in 1939.

The first order given to Goodyear was for "K" class airships, and over 100 were produced by 1943. The "K" ships were successful ASW craft, and out of a total of 135 only one was lost to enemy action, though before it crashed into the sea it succeeded in putting the enemy submarine out of action. It is claimed by the U.S. Navy that no vessel in a convoy escorted by these airships was lost through enemy action during the last war.

The post-war development saw a marked improvement in the design and operational capabilities of the Goodyear-built airships. The navy airships of the 1950s were bigger than any non-rigid craft built previously and also possessed outstanding military attributes. The *ZP2N1*, for example, was the first U.S. Navy ship specifically designed to be refuelled in flight, and the *ZP3K* was designed for operation from aircraft carriers (most airships were capable of being refuelled in flight and certainly many airships had landed on aircraft carriers previous to the *ZP3K*), while airships built later were capable of increased speed and endurance capacity.

On 25 May 1954 a ZPG-2 airship achieved an endurance record by staying airborne from 17 to 25 May, a total of eight days and eight hours (200.2 hours), carrying a full crew and an operational load. This record was beaten by another ZPG-2 ship in 1957. The ship stayed aloft from 4 to 15 March, completing a return trip to Spain in eleven days (264.12 hours). The distance covered with a full crew and an operational load was 9,448 miles.

The last and largest of the non-rigid airships used by the U.S. Navy was the Goodyear-built "ZPG-3W" class. Five of these were produced, one of which was lost while engaged on a search and rescue mission, and the last phased out of naval service in 1961. The main task of the "ZPG-3W" class was as Airborne Early Warning craft, and, as such, they were equipped with the, then, latest electronic detection equipment. The envelope of these airships served as a radome for a 40-foot internally-mounted radar antenna system, and the cars were supported by a system of steel cables laced through the top and bottom of the rubberised-fabric envelope.

The cars of the large navy airships of the 1950s were all constructed from a sandwich-type material known as "Bondolite". This material was made by facing a balsa wood core with sheets of aluminium-alloy; the "Bondolite" was then fixed to the metal framework of the car, which was built in several assemblies and then joined together.

Ex-*K28*, sister ship to *Puritan II*

The Wingfoot Express had engines suspended from the envelope aft of the car

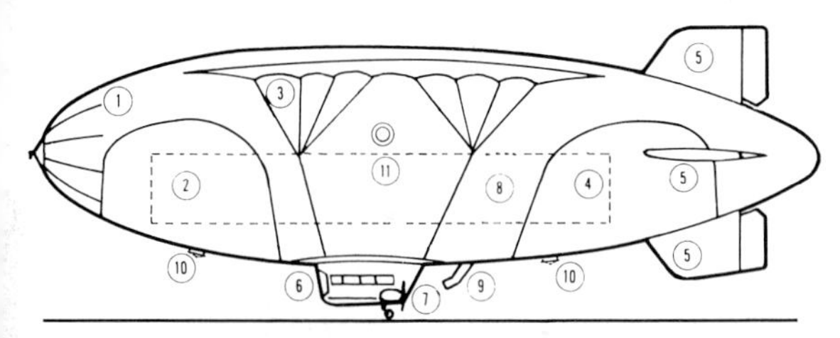

The component parts of a modern Goodyear non-rigid airship: (1) nose cone supports; (2) forward ballonet; (3) catenary curtain and suspension cables; (4) aft ballonet; (5) rudders and elevators; (6) car; (7) engines; (8) night sign lamps; (9) air scoops; (10) air valves; (11) helium valve

Mayflower III

In February 1968, Goodyear initiated a $5 million expansion programme for its airship operations, which included the provision of a new base at Houston, Texas, modernisation of the *Mayflower III* and *Columbia II*, based at Miami and Los Angeles respectively, and construction of a new airship, named *America*. This latter ship, completed in 1969, was built at Wingfoot Lake, near Akron, from where she made her first flight on 25 April 1969. She is currently based at Houston.

In 1971, a decision was made to build a fourth non-rigid airship for public relations operations in Europe in 1972. Components for the construction of the airship were flown from Akron to the Royal Aircraft Establishment at Cardington in Bedfordshire, and this airship, named *Europa*, made its first flight at Cardington on 8 March 1972.

During the winter months of each year, the *Europa* operates from a base which has been established at Capena in Italy. To accommodate the *Europa* and ground support vehicles, and to provide office space, crew quarters and adequate facilities for maintenance of the airship, a hangar has been erected at Capena. This concrete, steel and glass structure is 250 feet in length, 160 feet 9 inches wide and 90 feet in height. During the spring and summer months, the *Europa* tours Western Europe.

Europa

The envelope of the *Europa*, which has a surface area of 21,600 square feet, is made of two-ply Neoprene-coated Dacron, and like her sister ships is inflated with helium. On each side of the envelope is a four-colour sign consisting of 3,780 lamps which can flash static or animated messages. This can be read at a distance of one mile when the airship is cruising at a height of 1,000 feet. A turbojet APU, mounted in a removable pad on the undersurface of the ship's

Columbia III

The *Europa* at Cardington

Columbia IV, the replacement for *Columbia III*

gondola, drives a 500A 28V generator to supply electrical power for the signs and their control equipment. The turbojet is designed to operate without developing any appreciable amount of forward thrust for the airship.

The car, attached to the undersurface of the envelope, has accommodation for a pilot and six passengers, and has a single non-retractable landing wheel mounted beneath it.

The power consists of two 210 h.p. Continental 10-360-D six-cylinder horizontally-opposed air-cooled engines, each driving a Hartzell two-blade metal reversible-pitch pusher propeller. Standard tankage is provided for 138 U.S. gallons of fuel, and auxiliary tankage for 158 U.S. gallons. Total available fuel capacity is therefore 296 U.S. gallons. The volume of the envelope is 202,700 cubic feet.

By 1 January 1975 the *Europa* had flown 4,000 hours and carried more than 20,000 passengers since its first flight in 1972.

Columbia IV

Columbia IV, which is an identical replacement for *Columbia III*, was assembled at Goodyear's base at Houston, Texas in 1975. This new airship is 192 feet long, 59 feet high and 50 feet wide, and the new ship is to be operated on the same lines as her sister ships.

In six years of operation, the old *Columbia* has flown for more than 10,200 hours and, during that time, the ship flew more than 306,000 miles at an average speed of 30 m.p.h. This is the average lifetime and endurance of a Goodyear airship. The old ship was dismantled and her parts are at the Goodyear Aerospace Corporation in Akron for refurbishing and storage for later use.

Aereon III

This unique rigid airship is made up from three hulls linked by aerofoil-shaped centre sections extending almost the full length of the craft. There is an elevon control surface on the trailing-edge of each centre section, and a fin and rudder assembly under the rear of each outer hull. A small steerable tail-wheel is mounted under each fin. The retractable nose-wheel on the centre hull is carried on an extending leg, enabling the airship's angle of attack to be varied for take-off.

The cross-section of each hull is a regular twenty-sided polygon. The structure consists of transverse frames and stringers, but geodetic bracing is employed for a high strength-to-weight ratio. The

The triple-hulled airship, *Aereon III*

outer hulls are supported by girder spars passing through the centre hull. Most of the structure is of welded aluminium alloy, with steel used in some highly-stressed areas. A twin wall covering is used, with an outer skin of Tedlar plastic, 1/1,000 of an inch thick, separated from the inner wall of nylon by an airspace of one inch. Eighteen Mylar cells contain the helium lifting gas.

Aereon 26, an experimental "lifting body" airship, landing at NAFEC on 6 March 1971

A crew of two is carried at the front of the centre hull. The power plant is mounted at the rear of the centre hull, and is a shaft-turbine, driving a two-blade Helicom reversible-pitch rotor/propeller, with a diameter of 21 feet and blade chord of 8 inches. The power plant is also used to superheat the helium.

In addition to providing forward and reverse thrust, the rotor/propeller is tiltable with respect to the longitudinal axis of the hulls, thus providing control in pitch and direction.

Overall width is 56 feet, and the maximum diameter of each hull is 18 feet. The weight empty is 2,800 lb., and the ceiling is an altitude of 8,500 feet. Endurance is about four hours.

This airship is a model of a projected airship with a payload of 90 tons. The full-scale model would have a length of 400 feet and a diameter of 70 feet. Power would be by four 1,000 h.p. diesel engines, giving a speed of 150 m.p.h. The ultimate goal was to use a number of similar ships to provide low-cost transportation for unusual types of cargo. However, financial problems curtailed the Aereon experimental programme, and *Aereon III* is now in store.

Aereon 26

This hybrid "proof-of-concept" research vehicle is described as having the hull geometry of a lifting body airship. Only limited details are available at present, and the main points of interest can be found under Aereon in the tables on U.S. private airships.

Conrad Airship Corporation

This company was founded by Mr Conrad and his son to build a "medium-sized" rigid airship. Work on this airship was in progress early in 1975.

The hull is constructed of light alloy tubing, with ten ring formers and twelve longitudinal stringers. Lift will be provided by ten gas bags fabricated from laminated Mylar. The airship is to carry liquid ballast which is to be distributed and/or disposed of by high-volume transfer pumps.

The power plant is to consist of two 500 h.p. liquid-cooled engines, with the drive to the three propellers (of which one is on the axis of the airship at the tail) via two hydraulic units, each weighing 85lb. The range of the airship will be about 3,000 miles.

Tucker T X-1/Silver Hawk

The Californian Tucker Airship Company is constructing a small semi-rigid airship which is designated *T X-1*. It is planned to inflate this airship with hydrogen, and power it with one 90 h.p. McCullock aircooled engine.

The TX-1, later to be named *Silver Hawk*, is to fly as an experimental vehicle, and as such it will be fitted with three equipment bays for the installation of a "black box" and other experimental devices.

An interesting feature of the TX-1 is to be a "newly developed" one-man mooring system.

The Tucker Airship Company propose to build craft up to 350 feet in length after the TX-1 is tested.

Raven STARship

This hot-air airship is known as the *STARship*, STAR representing Small Thermal Airship by Raven. Designed by Raven, and built at the factory of Raven Industries at Sioux Falls, South Dakota, she made her first flight in the U.S.A. on 7 January 1975, and was named *Verkehrshaus Luzern* in Switzerland, on 13 May 1975.

The ship has cruciform inflated tail surfaces. The aft portion of the lower vertical surface is movable and serves as a rudder, and the aft section of each horizontal tail surface is also movable, serving as an

TX-1, or *Silver Hawk*, under construction

elevator to assist pitch control. The ship has tubular metal skids and accommodates a crew of two as well as the dual 11 million BTU propane burner, 80 to 100 Imperial gallons of liquid propane, 100 lb. of baggage and the power plant. The power plant is a Revmaster conversion of a Volkswagen motor car engine and drives a shrouded propeller which is five feet in diameter. The pitch of this propeller is ground-adjustable. A four-stroke APU is used to maintain the pressure within the envelope at .05 lb/sq.in. The gross weight is 2,400 lb, and the ship's ceiling is 4,920 feet.

Remotely Piloted Mini Blimp (RPMB)

Developmental Sciences, Inc. of California demonstrated a mini-RPMB early in the autumn of 1974 near Los Angeles. The craft, shown in its urban surveillance role, took off "heavy" carrying 3½lb of payload, including a cine camera. Thus, the practicality of flight control, launch and recovery was demonstrated, as well as the photographic coverage possible with this craft. The envelope fairing was of ripstock nylon and Mylar, and a gimballed model aeroplane engine was used for propulsion and control.

The mini-RPMB is a smaller version of the craft, to be produced for traffic monitoring and other surveillance purposes. In fact, it will be a low-altitude platform equipped with television cameras or scientific monitoring instruments. The proposed length of this craft is 55 feet and the diameter 13 feet 6 inches. This gives a fineness ration of 3.85.

The thermal *Starship* developed by Raven Industries

A prototype RPMB surveillance airship being demonstrated near Los Angeles, California

The envelope for the RPMBs would be of two-ply Mylar-coated Dacron which would be supplied by the Goodyear Aerospace Corp. The envelope would have a volume of 5,500 cubic feet and be inflated with helium. The weight of the envelope would be 60lb and the weight of the other component parts of the ship would be 190 lb, thus giving a gross operational weight of 250lb.

Depending on endurance requirements, the RPMB would be powered by engines from 12 to 35 h.p. These engines would give top speeds of approximately 50 to 70 m.p.h.

An RPMB would cost about $40,000, exclusive of the fixed and mobile automatic mooring towers from which these small non-rigid craft are designed to operate.

U.S. PRIVATE AIRSHIPS

Class/Name	Make/Type	Launched	Vol. (cu.ft.)	Dimensions (ft) Length	Diam.	Engines No.(hp each)	Speed max. mph	Remarks
August Greth	August Greth (NR)	1903	—	—	—	—	—	One ascent made over San Francisco Bay *circa* 1903.
Leo Stevens	Leo Stevens (NR)	1903	—	—	—	—	—	The first ascent of this ship was made at Coney Island.
California Arrow	T.S. Baldwin (NR)	1904	8,000	52	17	1 Curriss (7)	—	Made at least four flights.
Meteor	T.C. Benbow and H.J. Wells (NR)	1904	14,000	74	21	1 4-cycle (10)	—	Had two four-bladed feathering paddle wheels.
Prosper Lambert	Hippolyte François (NR)	1904	65,000	150	40	1 (30)	—	Made one flight only 14.11.04. Had four screw propellers.
Morrell	National Airship Co. (NR)	1908	444,325	519.75	35.32	6 Hansen (30)	—	Lost pressure and crashed on trial flight.
America I/Polar Ship	Wellman-Goddard (NR)	—	224,155	165.9	(width 52.8)	1 Clement (25) (later 1 Ford (25))	18.5	Sponsored by a Chinaman. Unsatisfactory due to engine vibrations.
America IA	Wellman-Vaniman-Mallet (NR)	1907	275,340	186.1	(width 52.8)	1 Lorrain-Dietrich (80)	18.5	Ran into snow storm on first flight and was damaged on landing.
America IB (enlarged IA)	Vaniman (NR)	1910	345,000	231	(52.8)	2 Lorrain-Dietrich (80)	24.5	Abandoned on attempt to cross the Atlantic.
Goodale	Goodale (NR)	1909	8,000	58	—	1 (7)	—	Built and piloted by a boy, Frank B Goodale of Toledo. Made a number of successful flights. Similar to *Santos Dumont No. 9*.
Akron	— (NR)	1912	345,940	260	47 (width 49.5)	2 (100); 1 (80); 1 (17)	—	Exploded on Atlantic crossing attempt because of faulty valves. Vaniman and four others killed.
Pasadena	Knabenshue (NR)	1913	75,231	151.1	(width 30.36)	1 Hansen (30)	31.5	A joy riding ship designed by C.F. Willard.

U.S. PRIVATE AIRSHIPS

Class/Name	Make/Type	Launched	Vol. (cu.ft.)	Dimensions (ft) Length	Diam.	Engines No.(hp each)	Speed max. mph	Remarks
Wingfoot Express (FD Type)	Goodyear (NR)	1919	95,000	162	(width 33.44)	2 Gnome La Rhône rotary engines	—	Crashed after six flights on 21.7.19.
Pony Blimp A	Goodyear (NR)	1919	35,350	95.5	28 (height 40)	1 Ace pusher (40)	40	Weight empty 1,460lb. Gross lift 2,390lb. Useful lift 930lb.
O.A.1	Goodyear/Pony Blimp (NR)	1920	35,350	95	28	1 Lawrence (50)	45	First two sold to commercial organisations and the third lost with *Naval D I* in a fire at Wingfoot lake. Three built.

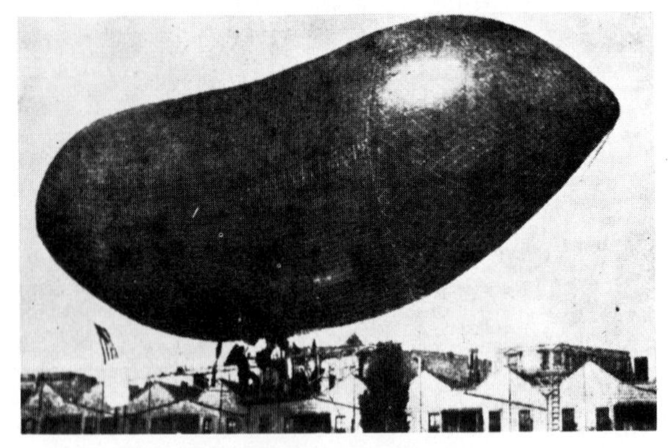

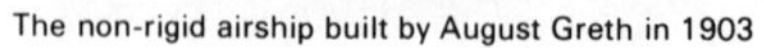

The non-rigid airship built by August Greth in 1903

Leo Stevens' airship at Coney Island in 1903

Class/Name	Make/Type	Launched	Vol. (cu.ft.)	Dimensions (ft) Length	Diam.	Engines No.(hp each)	Speed max. mph	Remarks
Pilgrim	Goodyear (NR)	1925	47,700	105.5	31	1 Lawrence (60)	50	Ultimate development of the *Pony Blimp*. Used hydrogen then helium. Was the forerunner of all succeeding Goodyear ships.

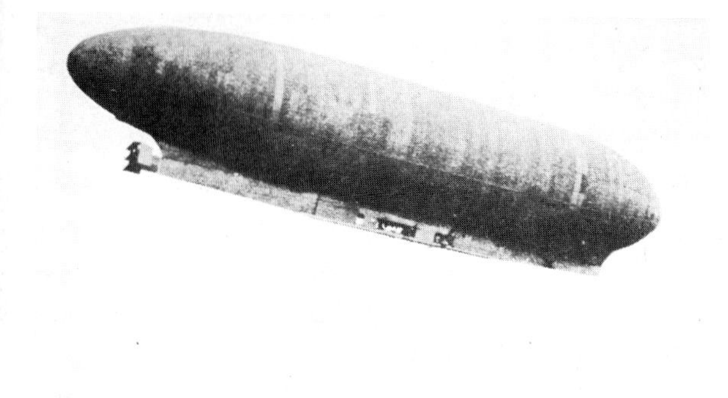

The *Akron* exploded on an attempted Atlantic crossing in 1912, because, it is stated, her valves were not made large enough

The *Pasadena* which was designed by C.F. Willard in 1913

The basket of the Albatross.

T.S. Baldwin's *SC-1* which was built for the U.S. Army. Baldwin's *California Arrow* took part in the St Louis Exhibition of 1904, and he is also reported to have built about 12 other ships.

Brain Bowland's hot-air airship *Albatross* photographed in Flight during her third inflation in 1975.

U.S. PRIVATE AIRSHIPS

Class/Name	Make/Type	Launched	Vol. (cu.ft.)	Dimensions (ft) Length	Diam.	Engines No.(hp each)	Speed max. mph	Remarks
Pilgrim (enlarged)	Goodyear (NR)	1929	55,000	110	32	1 Lawrence (60)	50	Last flight 10.12.31.
Defender	Goodyear (NR)	1929	179,000 (later 183,000)	184	44	2 WWW (165)	63	Became Naval *G1* in September 1935.
Puritan (Volunteer, Mayflower, Vigilant, Neponset)	Goodyear (NR) TZ	1928-30	86,000	128	36	2 Siemens Halska (70-80)	—	Sold to private concerns. *Neponset* wrecked.
Puritan (Volunteer)	Goodyear (NR)	1929-31	96,000	133	39	2 (125)	60	*Puritan* destroyed in full gale at Springfield.
Heinen Air Yacht	Heinen Air Yacht Corp. (NR)	1930	36,600	104	25 (height 39)	1 Brounback Tiger (90-100)	—	Crashed while landing on 16.2.31.
Volunteer II (Mayflower I, Vigilant, Mayflower II, Columbia, Reliance, Puritan, Volunteer)	Goodyear (NR)	1932	112,000	141	39	2 Warner Scarabs (125)	60	*Vigilant* wrecked and parts used for *Columbia*. *Mayflower I* wrecked in gale.
Enterprise I (Puritan, Resolute, Reliance, Rainbow L7, Ranger L2, Replacement Ranger, Ranger Ex-18, Volunteer Ex-L19, Enterprise Ex-L16, Mayflower Ex-L14)	Goodyear (NR)	1934-47	123,000	148	46	2 Warner (145)	62-63	Useful lift 1,461lb.
Enterprise II Ranger III, Mayflower II	Goodyear (NR)	1946	123,000	148	46	2 Warner (145)	62-63	*Enterprise* had an experimental envelope in 1948.
Puritan II (Ex-K28)	Goodyear (NR)	1946	425,000	251.7	57.8	2 Pratt & Whitney (42)	77	Width 62.5ft; Height 79ft.
Mayflower III	Goodyear (NR)	1959	132,500	150	41	2 Continental (175)	61	Sister ship to *Columbia II*.
Columbia II	Goodyear (NR)	1963	147,000	157	41	2 Continental (175)	57	Christened on 19.8.63. Given second envelope in December 1966.

Class/Name	Make/Type	Launched	Vol. (cu.ft.)	Dimensions (ft) Length	Diam.	Engines No.(hp each)	Speed max. mph	Remarks
Aereon III	Aereon Corporation (R)	1965	40,000	85	—	1 Solar Titan (70)	65	Combination of aerostatic and aerodynamic lift. Success but not developed.
Aereon 26	Aereon Corporation (R)	1970	—	27.6	(span 22.4) (height 7.4)	1 McCulloch (90)	127	Research model.
Columbia III, America	Goodyear (NR) GZ20	1969	202,700	192	45.92	2 Continental (210)	50	Details for *America* are the same as for *Columbia III*.
Europa	Goodyear (NR) GZ20	1972	202,700	192	45.92	2 Continental (210)	50	First airship to be flown at Cardington since the *Bournemouth* in 1951-52.
Remotely Piloted Mini Blimp	Developmental Sciences, Inc. (NR)	1974	—	16	4.15	1 Model aeroplane engine (¼)	20	This is the demonstration model built by D.S.I. and is much smaller than the machines intended for surveillance purposes. Larger types of RPMB, such as "Traffic Eye", would have a buoyancy of 250lb, a fineness ratio of 3.85, and a volume of 5,500 cubic feet.
STARship	Raven Industries, Inc (NR)	1975	138,435	120.1	47.11	1 converted Volkswagen (65)	25	Thermal airship. First flight on 7.1.75. Gross lift 2,400lb. Useful lift 500lb. Ceiling 4,920ft. Balloon fabric consists of 2.9oz/yd^2 of urethane coated dacron. Named *Verkehrshaus Luzern* for a flight made in Switzerland.

Modified Goodyear ships are mentioned by the same name and are placed in chronological order.

U.S.A. PRIVATE AIRSHIPS

Class/Name	Make/Type	Launched	Vol. (cu.ft.)	Dimensions (ft) Length	Diam.	Engines No.(hp each)	Speed max. mph	Remarks
Columbia IV	Goodyear (NR)	1975	202,700	192	45.92	2 Continental (210)	50	Identical replacement for *Columbia III*.
Conrad	Conrad Airship Corp (R)	—	250,000	225	50	2 (500)	85	Reported to be building in the open air.
Tucker TX1/ Silver Hawk	Tucker Airship Co. (SR)	—	20,500	91	20 (height 26)	1 McCulloch (90)	55	Can be inflated with helium or hydrogen. Fineness ratio 4.4 to 1.
Albatross	B.J. Bowland (NR)	1975	140,000	112	(width 50) (height 65)	1 Rockwell (40)	—	Hot-air airship.
*								
American Eagle	Riggs and Rice (NR)	1910	35,000	100	25	1 Curtiss (34)	—	Also went under about six other names.
Anderson	Anderson (NR)	1910	—	—	—	—	—	Small non-rigid craft.
Bumbaugh	Bumbaugh and Fisher (NR)	1910	—	166	—	1 (35)	—	—
Dusevoir	— (NR)	1910	—	—	—	—	—	Small craft.
Hall	Myers (NR)	1910	—	—	—	—	—	Small craft.
Hill	Myers (NR)	1910	—	—	—	—	—	Small craft.
Honeywell	Keller (NR)	1910	30,000	—	—	—	—	—
Beachey	Knabenshue/Beachey (NR)	1910	—	47	14.6	1 (5)	—	Knabenshue model airship.
Nassr	— (NR)	1910	—	—	—	—	—	Small experimental craft.
Newstadt	Newstadt and Jacobs (NR)	1910	—	—	—	—	—	Small craft.
Strobel	C.J. Strobel (NR)	1912	8,000	58	—	1 (7)	—	A small airship used as a fairground demonstration model.
Whittesley	Whittesley (NR)	1910	—	—	—	—	—	Very small airship.
Wild	Wild (NR)	1910	—	—	—	—	—	Very small airship.
Zodiac V	Zodiac III-type (NR)	1910	49,440	134	28	1 (30)	—	—

* *The airships mentioned in the above table were either fairground or experimental craft.*

D-2, which was transferred to the U.S. Navy. For full details see under U.S. Naval airships

An OA1-type Pony Blimp, built by Goodyear for the U.S. Army

TC-7 being used for aeroplane hook-on experiments. This ship had two single ballonets, whereas *TC-4*, *TC-5* and *TC-6*, had only one double ballonet

TC-5. The cars of *TC-1* to *TCII* were identical to the Navy's *J3* car

The *TC-10* had more power at her disposal than earlier ships of the "TC" class, and was able to reach speeds of about 65m.p.h.

The U.S. Army's semi-rigid airship *RS-1*

RN-1, originally built for the French Navy, but she became a U.S. Navy ship before finally being taken over by the U.S. Army

The U.S. Army's modified AA-type Pony Blimp, *OB1*, originally the U.S. Navy's H-1. This motorised observation balloon was built about 1922 by Goodyear, and one of the class seems also to have been built by Airships Inc.

AC-1 was based on the design of the Pony Blimp, but with an elongation ratio of 3 to 6 her aerodynamic stability was very poor

U.S. ARMY AIRSHIPS

Class/Name	Make/Type	Launched	Vol. (cu.ft.)	Dimensions (ft) Length	Diam.	Engines No.(hp each)	Speed max. mph	Remarks
Pony Blimp/OA	Goodyear (NR)	1920	35,350	95.5	28	1 Lawrence (50)	40	Four built. Intended for employment as motorised kite balloons.
OB1 (ex-U.S.N. "H" class)	Goodyear (NR)	1922	43,030	94.8	30.8	1 Lawrence (50)	45	Modified *Pony Blimp* (*AA*) used as a motorised observation balloon. Four of this class bought by the army.
MA (AG1)	Goodyear (NR)	1922	180,000	169	48	2 AM U6D (135)	65	Based on the *Pony Blimp*. Aerodynamic stability not good.
MB	Goodyear (NR)	—	—	—	—	—	—	Motorised kite balloon. One built.
A4	Goodyear (NR)	1919	95,000	162	33.5	1 Curtiss (90)	46	Fuel tank placed outside the envelope. Modelled on Naval "E" and "F" classes.
TA1-5	Goodyear (NR)	1923	130,600	162	39.3	2 Curtiss OX5	—	Weight empty 5,671lb. Useful lift 1,871lb.
TE1-2	Airship Inc and Aircraft Dev. Corp. (NR)	1926	80,200	136	34	2 Lawrence (40)	45	Built to replace "TA" class in order to save helium.
TF1	Airship Inc and Aircraft Dev. Corp. (NR)	1926	52,290	106	30.9	1 Lawrence (40)	40	Weight empty 1,937lb. Useful lift: 933lb.
RN1	Zodiac (NR)	1921	326,500	264	49.5	2 Renault (250)	49	Built for French Navy to carry ASW weapons. Became U.S. Navy *ZD*, then handed over to U.S. Army.
RS1	Goodyear (SR)	1926	745,000	282	86	4 Liberty (300)	70	Trim tests carried out 19.4.26. The engines were carried in two power cars.
TC1, 2 and 3	Goodyear (NR) *TC1* by Airships Inc.	1922	200,600	196	44.5	2 Wright "1" (150)	52	Advanced training ships, for helium inflation. Replaced "C" and "D" classes. *TC3*

U.S. ARMY AIRSHIPS

Class/Name	Make/Type	Launched	Vol. (cu.ft.)	Dimensions (ft) Length	Diam.	Engines No.(hp each)	Speed max. mph	Remarks
								made the first hook-on experiments with a Sperry Messenger on 15.12.24. *TC1* destroyed by fire in June 1923.
TC4 and 5	Airships Inc. (NR)	1924	200,600	196	44.5	2 Wright "1" (150)	52	*TC5* used in aeroplane release experiments 3.10.24.
TC6	Airships Inc. (NR)	1924	200,600	196	44.5	2 Lawrence (190)	58	Weight empty 4,073lb. Useful lift 4,073lb.
TC7, 8 and 9	Goodyear (NR)	—	200,600	196	44.5	2 Lawrence (190)	—	These ships had the same basic characteristics as *TC4, 5* and *6* but had two single ballonets instead of one.
TC10, 11 and 12	Goodyear (NR)	1932	219,000	214	—	2 (200)	65	*TC1* to *11* had cars identical to the U.S. Navy *J3* airships.
TC13	Goodyear (NR)	—	360,000	233	54	2 Pratt & Whitney (375)	77	Became a naval airship in 1937.
TC14	Goodyear (NR)	—	380,000	233	54	2 Pratt & Whitney (375)	75	Two ballonets. Became a naval airship in 1937 when the U.S. Army ceased all airship operations.

TC-14, later to become a Naval airship, landing at Scott Field, Illinois

U.S. Navy Non-Rigid Airships

The U.S. Navy employed non-rigid airships from 1917 until the Naval Airship Service was disbanded in 1961. However, even though non-rigid craft were in use throughout the life of the Airship Service, their popularity declined with the advent of the U.S. Navy's rigid airships. Though, sad to say the tragic loss of the *Akron* and *Macon* was partially responsible for the accelerated development of non-rigid airships, particularly for the U.S. Navy.

In spite of this increased activity, the U.S. Navy had only ten non-rigid airships in operation when Pearl Harbor was attacked on 7 December 1941. By the end of the war, 168 navy airships were in operation, most of which were manufactured by Goodyear. In fact, a few of Goodyear's commercial fleet of airships were taken over by the navy to serve mainly as training craft.

The U.S. Navy airships accrued an incredible record during the war, especially in the role of ASW escorts for convoys. In the Atlantic and Gulf Coast Waters of the United States, and in the coastal waters of the Caribbean, Eastern Central America and Brazil, 532 vessels in all were sunk, but not one vessel was sunk by enemy submarine action while under escort by an airship. Altogether, naval airships escorted 89,000 ships during the war without the loss of a single ship. One of the most astonishing feats carried out by a navy airship was the capture of the German submarine *U-858*, which surrendered to the U.S. Navy off Cape May, N.J., after being escorted by the airship for 1,000 miles. A boarding party from USS ATR-57 was put aboard the U boat in May 1945.

After the Second World War the U.S. Navy reduced its airship operations but, with the outbreak of the Korean war, these were again stepped up.

The last airships built for the U.S. Navy were the four huge ZPG-3W type non-rigid airships built by Goodyear. These airships were for use in the American early-warning defence network, but were retired from service when more sophisticated early warning equipment was developed.

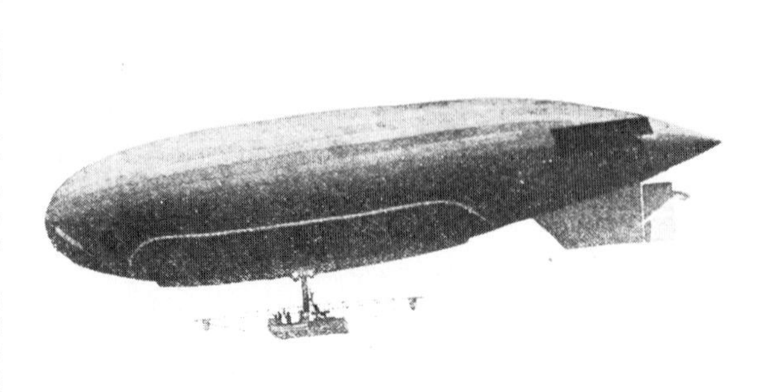

A1 (DN1), the semi-rigid ship built for the U.S. Navy in 1917

More information on the U.S. Navy Airship Service can be found in the entry for Goodyear airship operations.

One of the Navy "C2" class ASW airships which was taken over by the U.S. Army

The U.S. Navy's Airship *E1* with a handling party. The fuel tanks were placed inside the envelope between the ballonets

One of the U.S. Navy's "F" class ships. The 125 h.p. Union engine can be seen mounted on the rear of the car

G 1, formerly the *Defender* of the Goodyear fleet. As *Defender* her volume was 178,000 cubic feet, but she was given a new envelope and as *G1* her volume was 183,000 cubic feet

The car of a "C2" class ship. With two engines and a greater range of operation, these ships were designed to be much more reliable than previous ships. Note the two blowers, and the Eta-type suspension patches

J 4 on patrol. When the U.S. Army ceased airship operations in 1937 *J 4* was returned to the Navy and was stationed at Lakehurst

K2 damaged after a slight mishap

The training airship *L 3*. Immediately after the raid on Pearl Harbor, five Goodyear L-ships were turned over to the U.S. Navy and for a time were used on anti-submarine patrols

A "ZPK" class airship — better known as a K-ship — photographed during take-off. During the Second World War about 134 of these ships were constructed

K 124 bearing U.S. Naval Reserve markings. This patrol craft was assigned to the Naval Airship Reserve Training Unit at Lakehurst, N.J. in December 1947. The only other Reserve Unit was located at Santa Anna in California

U-858, surrendering to the U.S. Navy off Cape May in 1945, after being escorted by a Destroyer Escort for 1,000 miles. A U.S. Navy airship provides cover overhead as a boarding party from USS ATR-57 is being put aboard

A stern view of a "ZS ZG 1" airship, showing the inverted Y fins

On board a K-ship during the Second World War. K-ships were crewed by three officers and seven ratings

A "ZPG-Z" ship photographed during take-off. The stabilising X fins and "ruddervators" on the stern are mounted at a 45 degree angle from the vertical and horizontal instead of the more common 90 degree angle

U.S.NAVY

U.S.NAVY

N 1, later to become a "ZPG-2" ship. This prototype had her inboard engines arranged so that one engine could drive both propellers. This was the first ship to have X fins

M 1 (*XM 1*). Twenty-two of the "M" class were ordered during the last war but owing to an improvement in the U-boat situation only four were completed

The last and largest class of non-rigid airships built for the U.S. Navy were the "ZPG-3W" ships. The ship in the photograph is on a mobile mast outside the vast airship shed at Akron

U.S. NAVY NON-RIGID AIRSHIPS

Class/Name	Make/Type	Launched	Vol. (cu.ft.)	Dimensions (ft) Length	Diam.	Engines No.(hp each)	Speed max. mph	Remarks
A1 (DN1)	Connecticut Aircraft Co	1917	110,000	175	35 (height 50)	1 Sturtevant (140)	35	Maximum altitude 6,000 feet. Useful lift 1,604lb.
B1-20	Goodyear (9) Goodrich (5) Connecticut (2)	1917	84,000	163	31.5 (height 46)	1 Curtiss OXX3 (100)	47	Training and ASW ships. Crew of three.
C1-16	Goodyear/Goodrich	1918	181,000	196	42 (height 54)	2 Hispano Suiza (150)	60	A number of "C" ships were handed over to the U.S. Army. Mainly used for ASW.
D1-6	Goodyear	1919	190,000	198	42 (height 58)	2 Union (125)	58	Twenty ships ordered but only five accepted.
E1	Goodyear	1918	95,000	162	33.5	1 Thomas (150)	56	The fuel tanks of this ship were inside the envelope. Engine on rear of car.
F1	Goodyear	1919	95,000	162	33.5	1 Union (125)	52	Engine testing ships, with engine on the stern of the car. Altitude 8,000 feet.
G1 (ex-Defender), 2-8	Goodyear	1929 (As *Defender*)	196,000	190	45	2 Continental (220)	63.2	Had a volume of 178,000cu.ft. when new. *G1* had a new envelope fitted in September 1935. Ten ships ordered but *9, 10, 11* were cancelled.
H1-4 (Pony Blimps) Type A.B.	Goodyear	1922	43,030	94.8	30.8	1 Lawrence (50)	45	The "H" class was designed to be towed at 70m.p.h. A blower was considered to be essential, and to keep up pressure 1,000 engine revs were necessary. The performance under tow was considered good as the "H" handled much better than an "R"-type kite balloon. The

Class/Name	Make/Type	Launched	Vol. (cu.ft.)	Dimension (ft) Length	Diam.	Engines No.(hp each)	Speed max. mph	Remarks
								"H" was really a motorised kite baloon. The car of the "H" could be detached quickly. An elongation of 3 made the envelope inefficient. A navy "H" ship was destroyed in a fire along with *D6* in August 1921. The navy later transferred an "H" ship to the U.S. Army (See *OB1*).
J1	Goodyear	1922	173,000	170.5	45	2 Aero Marine WC (150)	—	Weight empty 7,000lb.
J3-4	Goodyear	1925(?)	212,000	—	—	—	—	*J4* reverted to the Army after loss of the *Macon* but when army gave up airships in 1937 it was returned to the navy.
K1	Goodyear	1931	320,000	220	54	2 (300)	75	The first NR to be fuelled with Blau gas.
K2	Goodyear	1938	404,000	246	(height 76)	2 Pratt & Whitney (350)	75	Served in WWII.
K3-8	Goodyear	1940	416,000	248.5	57.85	2 Wright (400)	72	Six of these ASW ships built.
K9-13	Goodyear	—	416,000	248.5	57.85	2 Pratt & Whitney (425)	—	Height 79 feet. Weight empty 17,600lbs.
K14-135	Goodyear	1943	425,000	251.7	57.8	2 Pratt & Whitney (425)	77	135 "K" ships were built during WWII. Carried crews of eight or ten.
ZP2K	Goodyear	1944	456,000	283	60	2 Pratt & Whitney (425)	79	Converted into *ZSG-3* and flown until 1955.
L 1-22 (Training Class)	Goodyear	(L5) 1934	123,000	150	46	2 Warner (145)	63	Seven of this class were originally Goodyear publicity airships. Altitude 9,000 feet.

U.S. NAVY NON-RIGID AIRSHIPS

Class/Name	Make/Type	Launched	Vol. (cu.ft.)	Dimensions (ft) Length	Diam.	Engines No.(hp each)	Speed max. mph	Remarks
M1-4 (XM1)	Goodyear	1943	625,000	287	66	2 Pratt & Whitney (500)	79	Twenty-two ordered but only four completed because of improvement in U boat situation.
XM1/Mighty Mick	Goodyear	—	725,000	308	68.3	2 Pratt & Whitney (550)	—	Airborne for 170hrs 17mins in 1946.
ZSG2	Goodyear	Post 1945	550,000	—	—	—	—	Eighteen built(?)
ZSG3 (ex ZP2K)	Goodyear	Post 1945	543,000	266	62	2 Pratt & Whitney (550)	75+	Number built unknown. *ZSG2* modernised to permit the installation of new equipment.
ZP3K	Goodyear	Post 1945	527,000	266.8	62.10	2 Pratt & Whitney (550)	—	Width 70 feet. Height 83.5 feet. Goodyear "K" ship.
ZSG4 1-15	Goodyear	1953	527,000	266.48	62.10	2 Pratt & Whitney (550)	75+	Flown until 1959. Replacement for "K" ships.
ZSG2G1.1-18 (ZP5K)	Goodyear	1954	670,000	285	68	2 Curtiss Wright (800)	—	Long duration ASW patrols. One of this class was flying, for experimental purposes, until 1961. Had three inverted Y fins.
N1/ZPG1	Goodyear	1951	825,000	324	71	2 Wright Cyclon (700)	—	Prototype of "N" class later to be designated as "ZPG2" class. This ship had inboard engines arranged so that one engine could drive both propellers. The *ZPG1* was the first ship to have X fins, which were known as "ruddervators".

Class/Name	Make/Type	Launched	Vol. (cu.ft.)	Dimensions (ft) Length	Diam.	Engines No.(hp each)	Speed max. mph	Remarks
ZPG2 1-12 (ex-"N" class)	Goodyear	1955	1,011,000	343	75	2 Wright (800)	—	Long distance ASW ships with X fins — "Ruddervators". Designed so one engine could drive both propellers for cruising under 40 knots.
ZPG2W 1-5	Goodyear	1955(?)	1,011,000	343	—	2 Wright (800)	81	Early Warning Radar ships. Engines placed inside the car.
ZPG3W 1-4	Goodyear	1958	1,516,300	403 (height 118)	85 (width 85.1)	2 Curtiss Wright (1,500)	80	Early Warning Radar ships. Deleted in 1962 when U.S. Naval Airship Service was disbanded. Ten men required for ground handling. Static lift 82,990lb. Dynamic lift 10,500lb. Useful lift 22,900lb. Gross lift 93,496lb.

The *Los Angeles*, ex-*LZ 126*, on the mast at Lakehurst

Rigid Airships of the U.S. Navy

In 1919, the U.S. Secretary of the Navy authorised plans for the construction of the rigid airships *ZR1*, known as the *Shenandoah*, and *ZR2*. The latter airship was built in England and was known there as the *R38*. The airship hangar at Lakehurst had not been completed at this time and so priority was given to the purchase of *R38*. Provision was also made for the training of U.S. Navy airship crews in England. The *R38* never reached America, as she crashed on her trial flights on 24 August 1921. In view of what subsequently became known of the *R38*, she was no loss, but the deaths of U.S. Navy personnel who were aboard her deprived the navy of many of its most experienced men. The British Airship Service also suffered greatly by losing its most experienced men.

The *R38* was not strong enough to withstand the stresses she endured while being put through her trial flights, but if she had been manned by a crew used to such a lightly built ship she might have survived.

The *Shenandoah* made her first flight on 4 September 1923, and remained in service until her destruction in a squall in September 1925. The ship suffered a number of exceptionally violent accidents during her career and also underwent many rigorous flights which, in all probability, weakened her structure and contributed greatly to her destruction. When the *Shenandoah* broke in two, her bow section rose to a height of 10,000 feet and by a miracle was brought down safely through the skill of one of the ship's officers. The stern section of the ship also made a balloon descent, and in all twenty-nine men survived out of a crew of forty-three.

The loss of the *Shenandoah* left *ZR-3*, the *Los Angeles*, as the only rigid airship on the navy inventory. This ship was obtained as compensation for the two Zeppelin craft which the United States

The *Shenandoah* in flight

should have received as wartime reparation, but these airships were destroyed by German airship crews to prevent them from passing into Allied (or other) hands. The *Los Angeles* was built by the Luftschiffbau Zeppelin Company, and was delivered to the United States on 15 October 1924. This rigid airship survived as a usetul craft until her retirement in 1932, when she became a "hanger queen" for a short time, and then was used for mooring mast experiments until she was finally broken up in 1940.

Akron and Macon

America's monopoly of helium ideally suited her to the development

Shenandoah moored to the mast on the USS *Patoka*

The wreck of the *Shenandoah*

USS *Akron* on the mast at Akron, Ohio

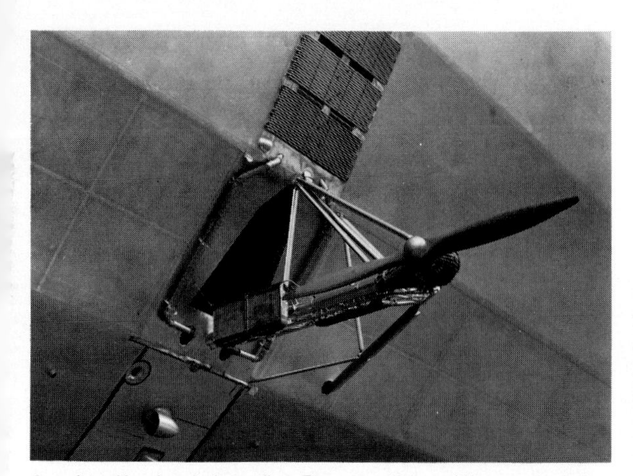

One of the *Akron's* swivel propellers. These propellers could be turned to deliver thrust either forward or astern; and vertical thrust, either up or down could also be delivered. One of the differences between the *Akron* and *Macon* was the installation of the radiators on the leading edge of the propeller outrigger; the *Macon's* were in streamlined housings on her hull

The nose of *Akron*, locked on the mooring out mast, emerges from the vast Goodyear Airdock at Akron, Ohio

of long-range rigid airships. These airships were designed as flying aircraft carriers for long-range naval patrol, particularly for combing the vast reaches of the Pacific, where, with the aid of aeroplanes, these lighter-than-air machines were to provide the justification for their existence.

In 1926, the 69th Congress of the United States authorised the U.S. Navy to build two rigid airships, and after two design competitions and the submission of thirty-seven designs, the contract was finally awarded to the Goodyear-Zeppelin Corporation on 6 October 1928.

Before these airships could be built, a special hangar, or airdock,

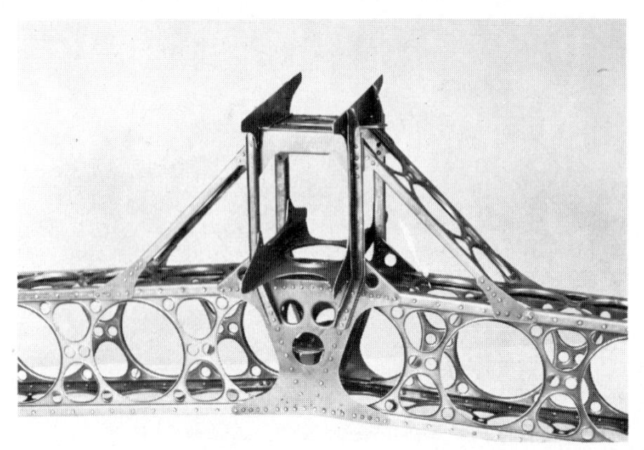

A part of one of the *Akron's* intermediate hull rings. The box-like structure carried one of the longitudinal girders

was constructed at Akron, Ohio. This hangar was completed in 1929, and is still regarded as the largest structure in the world without interior support. The hangar is 1,300 feet long, 300 feet wide, 200 feet high, and has semi-circular doors, aerodynamically designed to reduce wind currents and eddies which would make the handling of the big ships difficult and dangerous.

The *Akron* was christened with a great deal of ceremony on 8 August 1931, and her maiden flight was made on 25 September. She remained in service for about eighteen months and took part in a

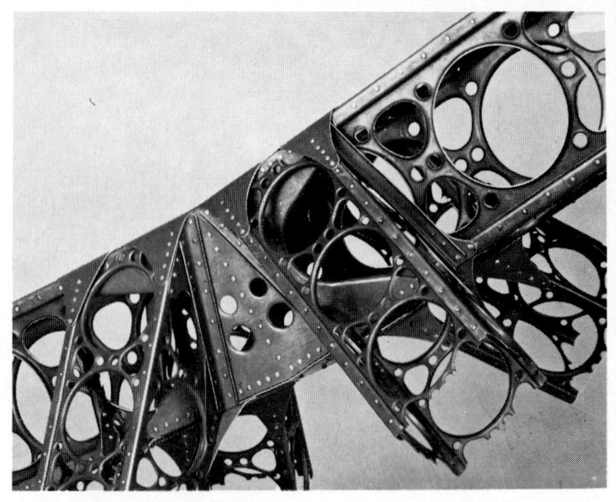

The junction of the Warren truss with the apex girder of one of *Akron's* main frames, showing riveting details

A close-up view of the *Akron's* tail. The four dark bands of "windows" partly around the circumference of the hull are the condensers of her water-recovery apparatus. Water recovered from the engine exhaust compensated for the loss of weight as fuel was used and thus eliminated the need to valve valuable helium

The Curtiss XF9C-1, piloted by Lieutenant Howard L. Young, caught on the *Akron's* skyhook on 3 May 1932, the first day that planes were operated from the ship's trapeze. The XF9C-1 is just about to be swung into the *Akron's* aeroplane compartment

number of U.S. Fleet exercises. In these she showed the value of her aeroplane carrying ability by launching fighter patrols, from her trapeze, in adverse weather conditions, which would have constituted a grave danger to the aircraft of the surface fleet.

The *Akron* was caught in a storm while cruising over the Atlantic on 4 April 1933, and was tossed about for about one and a half hours. On several occasions she was struck by severe turbulence, and then, eventually, her steering gear was damaged. After this she lost height rapidly and crashed into the ocean, where she was buffeted by the wind and waves and broken up. Only three of the *Akron*'s crew survived this disaster. A Board of Inquiry blamed the inexperience of the crew for the disaster and this judgement was vindicated by an examination of the *Akron*'s wreckage, which showed that the ship had not suffered any structural failure before the crash. However, a weakness was known to exist where the failure occurred, and it is known that repairs were delayed to allow the ship to go on manoeuvres. On 23 June 1933, only a short while after the crash of the *Akron*, her sister ship, the *Macon*, was commissioned into U.S. Navy service. With the exception of a few minor points *ZRS5*, the *Macon*, was a reproduction of the *Akron*, but her career was a much happier one, and even though her end was as violent it was slightly less tragic; two were killed out of a crew of 83.

For twenty-two months the *Macon* flew on navy manoeuvres, and spent a good deal of her time exercising and perfecting the operation of her five aeroplanes. However, tragedy struck on 12 February 1935 when the *Macon* was hit by severe turbulence while returning from naval manoeuvres over the Pacific. Her top fin was torn away, taking part of the hull with it and puncturing three gas cells, which then rapidly began to deflate. The *Macon* then shot up beyond her pressure height, to 4,850 feet, after being de-ballasted to a state of equilibrium, which allowed her engines to drive her so high. When above her pressure height, the automatic valves on all her gas cells

The skeletal framework of the *Macon*. Frame 170 has only just been put in position, ready for joining to the structure. An intermediate and a main frame can also be seen under construction in the foreground

USS *Macon* making her first landing at Sunnyvale, California, on 15 October 1933

opened and released a good deal of helium into the atmosphere, thus blowing away any remaining lift. The ship came down at a great rate, and only by jettisoning the remaining water ballast and slip tanks, and using the engines to brake her descent did the crew escape serious injury when she hit the water. An emergency landing was made, and the *Macon* slowly began to sink.

The loss of the *Macon* marked the end of the U.S. Navy's rigid airship programme, and the loss of the *Hindenburg* a few years later marked the end of this era with stark and brutal frankness.

The Metalclad Airship ZMC-2

This interesting experimental airship was built by the Aircraft Development Corporation which later became the Metalclad Airship Corporation. Development work started on *ZMC-2* in 1921, and by

A Curtiss F9C-2, piloted by Lieutenant D. Ward Harrigan, hooks on to the USS *Macon's* trapeze mechanism

1925 the Company had designed the airship and submitted a proposal to the U.S. Government. Following lengthy committee hearings, Congress appropriated $300,000 for the construction of what was to be the world's first successful all-metal airship and, on 18 August 1926, U.S. Navy officials signed a contract for the construction of the *ZMC-2*.

Testing of full size structural members and a full size stern section was carried out during 1927 and 1928, and eventually the U.S. Bureau of Aeronautics officially authorised the company to proceed with construction on 1 March 1928. The first rivet was driven in the

A head-on view of the metal-clad airship's car. The two 220 h.p. Wright Whirl Wind engines were capable of sustaining the ship at speeds of about 70 m.p.h.

U.S.NAVY
ZMC-2

bow section of the hull a few days later on 7 March. Construction work was completed in July of 1929, and the ship was inflated with helium by 10 August.

ZMC-2 completed all contract requirements to the complete satisfaction of the naval authorities, each trial being successful on the first attempt. The airship was then delivered to the U.S. Navy on 12 September 1929 and final tests were completed by the end of the month.

The airship was then in continuous operation until 1935 when she was "deflated" for a complete overhaul and inspection. The envelope was found to be in excellent condition with no serious deterioration of the "alclad" construction material noticeable.

ZMC-2, also known as the "Tin Bubble" was a great success and continued flying until 19 October 1939 — a long life by airship standards. Although the Corporation had plans for a larger metal-clad airship, nothing came of the project.

The general structural features of the metal airship can be summarised as follows: a series of rigid circular transverse frames, covered with thin duralumin, comprised the support for all weight loads, while the metal skin took tensile and sheer stresses. A small number of longitudinal members were also used.

The fin arrangement was composed of eight radially disposed surfaces. This was an unconventional pattern, but at least it gave good stability and control.

The metal envelope consisted of a laminated sandwich of duralumin, protected from corrosion on either side by a thin layer of aluminium. The combination of materials was called "alclad", and was lap-jointed with three staggered rows of rivets. In order to deal with the colossal number of rivets (over 3½ million), an automatic riveter, capable of inserting 5,000 per hour, was produced by the Corporation as early as 1925.

It is interesting to note that the *ZMC-2* was not popular among airship pilots as she was slightly unstable and caused air sickness on many occasions.

The metal-clad *ZMC-2* on arrival at Lakehurst on 12 September 1929. The "all clad" metal skin of the envelope was .0095 inches thick

U.S. NAVY RIGID AIRSHIPS

Class/Name	Make/Type	Launched	Vol. (cu.ft.)	Dimensions (ft) Length	Diam.	Engines No.(hp each)	Speed max. mph	Remarks
ZMC-2/Metalclad	Detroit Aircraft Co. (Hybrid)	1929	202,200	149.5	52.8	2 Wright Whirl Wind (220)	70	Envelope was a metal skin .0095in. thick holding two ballonets. Last flight 19.8.39.
ZR1/Shendoah	Govt.-built Zeppelin		2,150,000	680.5	78.74 (height 93.1)	6 Packard (357)	60	Broke in two in squall 3.9.25. Twenty gas bags.
ZR2/R38	R.A.W. Bedford	1921	2,724,000	695	85.6 (height 93)	6 Cossack (350)	70.6	Type "A" British Admiralty design. Fifteen gas bags. Designed for an altitude of 22,000 feet. Broke in two over Hull 24.8.21. Never delivered to the U.S. Navy. Crew of 49. Five survivors.
ZR-3 (LZ126)/ Los Angeles	Zeppelin Co., Germany	1924	2,471,700	656.6	90.5	5 Maybach (400)	68	The *Los Angeles* was used for mooring experiments towards the end of her career. Fourteen gas bags. Broken up 1939/40 after a successful career.
ZRS4/Akron	Goodyear	1931	6,500,000	758	132.9	8 Maybach (560)	83	These airships were known as the flying aircraft carriers of the U.S. Navy. Each ship could carry five aeroplanes. *Macon* had a better performance record than the *Akron*. The thrust of the swivel propellers on these ships was 6,000lb. up and 8,000lb. down for each propeller. Each ship had twelve gas bags. The gross lift of the *Macon* was
ZRS5/Macon	Goodyear	1933	6,500,000	785	132.9	6 Maybach (560)	83	

Class/Name	Make/Type	Launched	Vol. (cu.ft.)	Dimensions (ft) Length	Diam.	Engines No.(hp each)	Speed max. mph	Remarks
								403,000lb., her disposable lift was 160,644lb., and the weight of the ship when empty was 242,356lb. The *Akron* was lost at sea on 3.4.33 with 64 out of 66 crew members missing, and the *Macon* broke up over the Pacific Ocean on 12.2.35 with the loss of two crew members out of a total of 82 officers and men. Width of both ships 137 feet 5in., and height 146 feet 5in.

A stern view of the *ZMC 2*

Select Bibliography

Abbott, Patrick. *Airship: The Story of R.34 and the First East-West Crossing of the Atlantic by Air.* Adams & Dart, 1973

Aerostation, Vols 1-3. Journal of the Association of Balloon and Airship Constructors, USA, 1973-76

L'Aérostation Maritime et Ses Constructions 1914-18. Sous Secrétariat de L'Aéronautique Militaire et Maritime

Airships. Vickers Ltd., Airship Dept., Barrow-in-Furness

Amundsen, Roald and Ellsworth, Lincoln. *The First Flight Across the Polar Sea.* Hutchinson

Arnesen, Odd. *The Polar Adventure. The Italia Tragedy Seen at Close Quarters.* Victor Gollancz, 1929

Arnold, Henry H. *Airmen and Aircraft.* 1926

Beaubois, Henry and Demand, Carlo. *Airships: An Illustrated History.* Macdonald and Jane's, 1973

Bethuys, G. *Les Aérostiers Militaires.* H. Lecène et H. Oudin, 1889

Blakemore, Thos L. and Watters Pagon, W. *Pressure Airships.* Ronald Press, 1927

Bouttieaux, Général. *La Navigation par Ballons Dirigeables.* Librairie Ch. Delegrain

Braunbeck's Sport Lexikon: Automobilismus, Motorbootwesen, Luftfahrt. Verlag: Gustav Braunbeck, 1910-1913

Broke-Smith, P. W. C., Brigadier. *The History of Early Aeronautics.* Reprinted from the *Royal Engineers Journal*, March-June, 1952.

De Brossard, Captain. *Lachet Tous.* France Empire

Burgess, Charles P. *Airship Design.* 1927.

Collier, Basil. *The Airship: A History.* Hart-Davis MacGibbon, 1974

De Forest Chaudler, Charles and Diehl, Walter S. *Balloon and Airship Gases* 1926

Deeson, A. F. L. *An Illustrated History of Airships.* Spurbooks 1973

Dollfus, Charles and Bouché, Henri. *Histoire de L'Aéronautique.* "L'Illustration", 1942

Duz, Pyotr A. *The History of Aeronautics and Aviation in the USSR 1914-1918.* State Scientific — Technical Publishing House, Oborongiz, 1960

Eckener, Hugo, Dr. *Count Zeppelin, The Man and His Work.* Massie, 1938

Eckener, Hugo, Dr. *My Zeppelins.* Putnam, 1958

Ege, Lennart. *Balloons and Airships.* Blandford, 1974

Etève, A, Général. *Avant Les Cocardes.* Charles-Lavanzell

Flieger-Jahrbuch 1969. Chapter 17, 'Luftschiffahrt in Vergangenheit und Zukunft', by Ulrich Queck. Transpress VEB Verlag Für Verkehrswesen Berlin, 1968

De Forge, L. Sazerac, Capitaine. *La Conquête de L'Air en Dirigeable.* Berger-Levrault, 1910

Gamble, Snowden. *The Story of a North Sea Air Station.* Neville Spearman, 1967

Glaisher, James, Camille Flammarion, W. de Fonvielle and Gaston Tissandier. *Travels in the Air.* Richard Beutley & Son, 1871

Grierson, John. *Challenge to the Poles. Highlights of Arctic and Antarctic Aviation.* G. T. Foulis, 1964

Hartcup, Guy. *The Achievement of the Airship.* David & Charles, 1974

Henderson, Ernest F. *Germany's Fighting Machine.* The Bobbs-Merrill Co., 1914

Higham, Robin. *The British Rigid Airship 1908-1931.* G. T. Foulis, 1961

Hood, Joseph F. *The Story of Airships.* Arthur Barker, 1968

Hook, Thom. *'Shenandoah' Saga.* Air Show Publishers, 1973

Horton, Edward. *The Age of the Airship.* Sidgwick & Jackson, 1973

Hyth, Viscount and John Leyland. *The Naval Annual 1914.* William Clowes, 1914.

Investigation of Dirigible Disasters. Hearings Before a Joint Committee to Investigate Dirigible Disasters. Seventy-third Congress. May 22 to June 6, 1933. U.S. Government Printing Office, 1933

Jackson, Robert. *Airships.* Cassell, 1971

Jane's All The World's Aircraft. Jane's Yearbooks, 1909 to date

Jane's Freight Containers: Ports, Operators, Manufacturers. Jane's Yearbooks. 1970 to date

Jones, H. A. *The War in the Air. Official History of the War.* Oxford, 1937

Joux, Général. Un Dirigeable Militaire: L'Adjutant Vincenot. Blondel La Rougery, 1931

Kollman, Franz. *Das Zeppelinluftschiff: Seine Entwicklung Tätigkeit und Keistungen.* Verlag von M. Krayn, 1924

Lehmann, Ernst A. and Mingos, Howard. *The Zeppelins.* G. P. Putnam's Sons, 1927

Lehmann, Ernst A., Captain. *Zeppelin.* Lougmans, Green, 1973

Levitt, E. H. *The Rigid Airship.* Sir Isaac Pitman & Sons, 1925

Luschnath, H. *Zeppelin - Weltfahrten.* Vom ersten Luftshiff 1899 bis zu den Fahrten des *LZ 127 - Graf Zeppelin* - 1932. Dargesteltt in einer Sammlung von 264 echten Bromsilber - Bildern und einen Metallfolie - Bild der Weltflug - Gedenkmünze. Bilderstelle Lohse, 1933

McKinty, Alec. *The Father of British Airships: A Biography of E. T. Willows.* William Kimber, 1972

McPhee, John. *The Deltoid Pumpkin Seed.* Farrar, Straus and Girroux, 1973

Maitland, E. M., Air-Commador. *R.34.* Hodder and Stoughton, 1920

Manual of Remote Sensing. Chapter 8, 'Platforms', by Alden P. Colvocoresses. American Society of Photogrammetry, 1972

Meager, George F., Captain. *My Airship Flights* 19915-1930. William Kimber, 1970

Mooney, Michael M. *The Hindenburg.* Hart-Davis MacGibbon, 1972

Morpurgo, J. E. *Barnes Wallis: A Biography.* Longman, 1972

Nayler, J. L. and Ower, E. *Aviation of To-Day: Its History and Development.* Frederick Warne, 1930

Nobile, Umberto, General. *My Polar Flights, An Account of the Voyages of the Airships Italia and Norge.* Frederick Muller, 1961

Nobile, Umberto, General. *With Italia to the North Pole.* George Allen and Unwin, 1930

Official History of the War in the Air: World War I. HMSO

D'Orcy, Ladislas. *D'Orcy's Airship Manual: An International Register of Airships with a Compendium of the Airship's Elementary Mechanics.* The Century Co., 1917

Pratt, H. I. *Commercial Airships.* Nelson, 1920

Pritchard, J. Laurence, Captain. Editor, Aeronautical Reprints. Proceedings of The Royal Aeronautical Society.

Baker, J. F. *Secondary Stresses in Airship Hull Structures.* 1927

Cave-Brown-Cave, T. R., Wing-Commander. *The Machinery Installation of Airship R.101.* 1929

— *Safety from fire in Airships.* 1927.

Chitty, L. and Southwell, R. V. *A Contribution to the Analysis of Primary Stresses in the Hull of a Rigid Airship.* 1931

Fritsche, Carl B. *The Metalclad Airship.* 1930

Lyon, Hilda M. *The Strength of Transverse Frames of Rigid Airships.* 1930

Richmond, V. C., Lt-Col. *R.101*

Roxbee Cox, Harold. *The External Forces on an Airship Structure, with Special Reference to the Requirements of Rigid Airship Design*

Scott, G. H., Major. *Handling and Mooring of Airships.*

Poolman, Kenneth. *Zeppelins Over England.* White Lion Publishers, 1960

Rea, Alberto. 'Dirigibili Italiani Nella Grande Guerra'. *Rivista Aeronautica.* Vol. 1, January 1969

Riiser-Larsen, H. J. *Femti År For Kongen.* Gyldendal Norsk Forlag, 1957

Robinson, D. H. *Giants in the Sky: A History of the Rigid Airship.* G. T. Foulis, 1973

Robinson, Douglas. *The Zeppelin in Combat.* G. T. Foulis, 3rd edn, 1971

Robinson, Douglas H. *The LZ 129, Hindenburg.* Arco Publishing, 1964

Rosendahl, C. E. Lt Commander. *Up Ship.* Dodd, Mead & Co., 1932

Rosendahl, C. E. Lt Commander. *What About the Airship.* Charles Scribner's Sons, 1938

Roskill, S. W., Captain. *The Naval Air Service.* Vol. 1, 1908-1918. Navy Records Society, 1969

Santos-Dumont, Alberto. *My Airships: The Story of My Life.* Dover Publications, 1973. First published in French by Charpentier and Fasquelle, 1904, and first published in the English language by Grant Richards, 1904

Saundby, Robert, Air Marshal Sir. *Early Aviation: Man Conquers the Air.* Macdonald Library of the 20th Century, 1971

Sinlair, J. A., Captain. *Airships in Peace and War.* Rich & Cowoun, 1934

Sinclair, J. A. *Famous Airships of the World.* Frederick Muller, 1959

Shute, Nevil. *Slide Rule: The Autobiography of an Engineer.* William Heinemann, 1954

Smith, Richard K. *The Airships Akron & Macon: Flying Aircraft Carriers of the United States Navy.* United States Naval Institute, 1965

Sprigg, Christopher. *The Airship.* Samson, Low and Marston

Sumner, P. H. *The Science of Flight.* Technical Press

Technical Aspects of the Loss of the U.S.S. Shenandoah. Journal of the American Society of Naval Engineers. Vol.XXXVIII, No. 3, August 1926

"They Were Dependable" — Airship Operation World War II, 7 December 1941 to September 1945. Naval Airship Training and Experimental Command, U.S. Naval Air Station, Lakehurst, N.J., 1946

Tilgenkamp, Dr Erich, et al. *Schweizer Luftfahrt.* Zurich, 1942

Toland, John. *The Great Dirigibles: Their Triumphs & Disasters.* Dover Publications, 1972. First published as *Ships in the Sky: The Story of the Great Dirigibles* by Henry Holt, 1957

Upson, Ralph H. and de Frost Chandler, Charles. *Free and Captive Balloons.* 1926

Voyer, Hirschauer, Colonel. *Les Ballons Dirigeables.* Berger-Levrault

Walker, Percy B. *Early Aviation at Farnborough. The History of the Royal Aircraft Establishment.* Vol. 1: *Balloons, Kites and Airships.* Macdonald & Co. (Publishers) Ltd, 1971

Warner, Edward P. *Aerostatics.* 1926

Whale, G. *British Airships Past and Present.* Bodley Head

Whitehouse, Arch. *The Zeppelin Fighters.* Robert Hale, 1968

Williams, T. B., Captain. *Airship Pilot No. 28.* William Kimber, 1974

Index

Page numbers in bold type indicate an illustration.

A

B

M

N

O

P

T

U

V

W